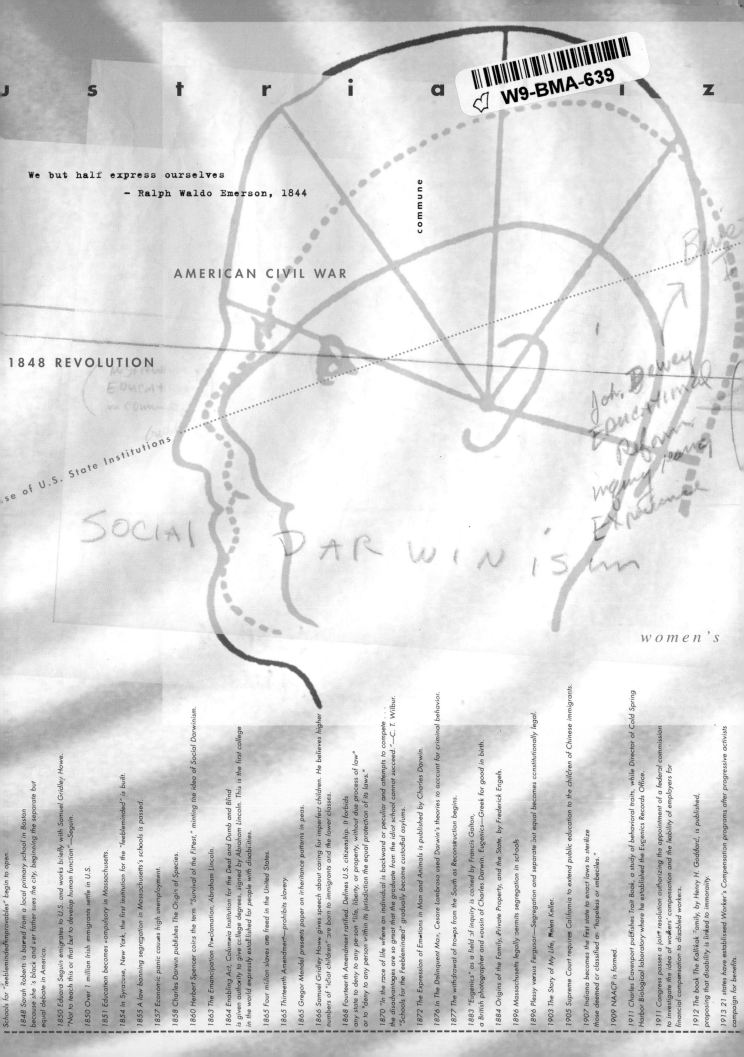

u s t r i a i z

We but half express ourselves
— Ralph Waldo Emerson, 1844

commune

AMERICAN CIVIL WAR

1848 REVOLUTION

...se of U.S. State Institutions

SOCIAL DARWINISM

John Dewey
Educational
Reform
many years
Experience

Blue

women's

Schools for "feebleminded-improvable" begin to open.

1848 Sarah Roberts is barred from a local primary school in Boston because she's black and her father sues the city, beginning the separate but equal debate in America.

1850 Edward Seguin emigrates to U.S. and works briefly with Samuel Gridley Howe. "Not to teach this or that but to develop human function"—Seguin.

1850 Over 1 million Irish immigrants settle in U.S.

1851 Education becomes compulsory in Massachusetts.

1854 In Syracuse, New York, the first institution for the "feebleminded" is built.

1855 A law banning segregation in Massachusetts's schools is passed.

1857 Economic panic causes high unemployment.

1858 Charles Darwin publishes The Origin of Species.

1860 Herbert Spencer coins the term "Survival of the Fittest," minting the idea of Social Darwinism.

1863 The Emancipation Proclamation, Abraham Lincoln.

1864 Enabling Act, Columbia Institution for the Deaf and Dumb and Blind is given authority to give college degrees, signed by Abraham Lincoln. This is the first college in the world expressly established for people with disabilities.

1865 Four million slaves are freed in the United States.

1865 Thirteenth Amendment—prohibits slavery.

1865 Gregor Mendel presents paper on inheritance patterns in peas.

1866 Samuel Gridley Howe gives speech about caring for imperfect children. He believes higher numbers of "idiot children" are born to immigrants and the lower classes.

1868 Fourteenth Amendment ratified. Defines U.S. citizenship. It forbids any state to deny to any person "life, liberty, or property, without due process of law" or to "deny to any person within its jurisdiction the equal protection of its laws."

1870 "In the race of life where an individual is backward or peculiar and attempts to compete . . . the disadvantages are so great that the graduate from the idiot school cannot succeed."—C. T. Wilbur. "Schools for the Feebleminded" gradually become custodial asylums.

1872 The Expression of Emotions in Man and Animals is published by Charles Darwin.

1876 In The Delinquent Man, Cesare Lombroso used Darwin's theories to account for criminal behavior.

1877 The withdrawal of troops from the South ends Reconstruction begins.

1883 "Eugenics" as a field of inquiry is coined by Francis Galton, a British photographer and cousin of Charles Darwin. Eugenics—Greek for good in birth.

1884 Origins of the Family, Private Property, and the State, by Frederick Engels.

1896 Massachusetts legally permits segregation in schools

1896 Plessy versus Ferguson—Segregation and separate but equal becomes constitutionally legal.

1903 The Story of My Life, Helen Keller.

1905 Supreme Court requires California to extend public education to the children of Chinese immigrants.

1907 Indiana becomes the first state to enact laws to sterilize those deemed or classified as "hopeless or imbeciles."

1909 NAACP is formed.

1911 Charles Davenport publishes Trait Book, a study of behavioral traits, while Director of Cold Spring Harbor Biological laboratory where he established the Eugenics Records Office.

1911 Congress passes a joint resolution authorizing the appointment of a federal commission to investigate the idea of workers' compensation and the liability of employers for financial compensation to disabled workers.

1912 The book The Kallikak Family, by Henry H. Goddard, is published, proposing that disability is linked to immorality.

1913 21 states have established Worker's Compensation programs after progressive activists campaign for benefits.

Becoming Citizens

Becoming Citizens

Family Life and the Politics of Disability

Susan Schwartzenberg

University of Washington Press

Seattle and London

Funded by the Office of Arts & Cultural Affairs,
City of Seattle.

University of Washington Press
P.O. Box 50096, Seattle, WA 98145
www.washington.edu/uwpress

Library of Congress Cataloging-in-Publication Data

Schwartzenberg, Susan.
Becoming citizens : family life and the politics of disability /
Susan Schwartzenberg.
        p. ; cm.
Includes bibliographical references.
ISBN 0-295-98519-4 (pbk. : alk. paper)
1. Parents of children with disabilities–Washington
(State)–Personal narratives.
2. Learning disabled children–Washington
(State)–Family relationships.
3. Special education–Parent participation–Washington (State).
4. Legal assistance to children–Washington (State). I. Title.
HQ759.913.S374 2005
649'.15–dc22   2005000390

All contemporary photographs by Susan Schwartzenberg
unless otherwise noted. Cover, The Nelson family c 1940.
Page x, Nelson Family, xeroxed page, courtesy of Linda
Nelson. Page xviii McNary Family trunk. Page xviv Hiramatsu
Family snapshot, c.1956, courtesy Mary Hiramatsu. All
other snapshots and documents courtesy of the families.

Contents

Becoming Citizens: Family Life and the Politics of Disability is a chronicle of the lives of thirteen families in the Seattle area who raised children with developmental disabilities between 1940 and 1980.

In January 2002 I began working with the Seattle Family Network, a small group of people connected to one another because they each have family members with a developmental disability. They came together to work with an artist to tell the story of the "senior families" in the disability community. This was a generation of parents who, after World War II, went against the conventional medical wisdom of that time and refused to institutionalize their children with significant developmental disabilities or "mental retardation." Growing up in the community, these children were often denied access to public schools, churches, programs, and medical benefits. At the heart of this document is the story of four mothers turned parent advocates, who, with grass-roots support from all over the country, became the principal authors of the Education for All Handicapped Children Act, passed as a Federal law in 1975. This civil rights legislation secures educational rights for every person with a disability in America.

This project explores through interviews and photographs the experience of family life and disability and the ways ordinary citizens become activists.

—Susan Schwartzenberg

Foreword

The City of Seattle Office of Arts & Cultural Affairs is honored to support *Becoming Citizens,* a collaboration between artist and photographer Susan Schwartzenberg and her partners in the disabilities community in Seattle. Believing in the critical importance of art in our civic life, the city has initiated and funded this and dozens of other projects through its innovative ARTS UP program, which supports community-artist teams in a collaborative process of exploration and creation.

Extending the parameters of contemporary public art practice, ARTS UP (Artist Residencies Transforming Urban Places) paired artists and communities to develop arts-based collaborations around shared goals. ARTS UP was an act of faith in the creative process and reinforced the notion that art could be at once community-based, challenging, and articulate. The program deployed the potential of arts in community change and development, grounded in the principles of cultural democracy, self-determination, collaborative cultural production, and social justice. ARTS UP sought to develop public infrastructure in support of arts-based civic dialogue, sustaining the City of Seattle's public art mission "to actively engage artists in the civic dialogue" and its goal of strong, healthy communities.

The ARTS UP model supposes a role for the artist that embraces his or her potential as a critical thinker and agent of change. The artistic results may cross disciplinary boundaries, so that their character as "art" may not even be readily apparent. Yet the artist's creative thinking, focus, and aesthetic are essential to such projects. Across the country, artists are engaging communities in this sort of generative process, compelled by the belief that art plays a vital role in civic life: that it can stimulate fresh ideas about old problems, give voice to citizens, and create a forum for group expression and action.

Becoming Citizens evidences the incredible power of this marriage between artistic practice and social agenda. As a work of art, *Becoming Citizens* combines a seductive elegance with the artist's critical observation and provocative juxtapositions. Schwartzenberg's identity as first an artist is readily apparent in both the book's visual articulation and its unlikely combination of materials and ideas. She brilliantly employs the power of the anecdote placed within the broad sweep of history, giving a compelling yet unsentimental face to the players in this important phase of the disability rights movement.

When employed to relate the story of the individual, art is a great leveler, communicating lived experience with a resonance and power that makes it our own. The testimonies and mementos juxtaposed in *Becoming Citizens* offer an evocative window into the hearts of these Seattle families, letting us walk in their shoes in a way that mere description could not. By excavating the evidence of this particular moment in time, Schwartzenberg has added it to the historical record in a way that invites participation from a broader public. The shared experience of storytelling incites us to lend our voices to the continuing struggle for social change.

Yet the work reaches out beyond art to many other disciplines as well, inviting a conversation with the fields of history, anthropology, medicine, and disability studies, to name a few. The exhaustive research engaged in by Schwartzenberg, the rigor she brought to her field interviews, and the incisive analysis that has led to this book can leave no doubt as to the relevance of her voice in these more concrete disciplines.

We are at a critical time in the development of community based art practice in this country, a time when the development of policies, infrastructure, and critical dialogue can coalesce the field, or their continued absence can evince its demise. Projects like this one contribute so much to the larger body of community-based art, greatly expanding our definition of the artist and opening windows of opportunity for artistic engagement with broader issues. The Office of Arts & Cultural Affairs has been proud to be part of that process of expansion through *Becoming Citizens.*

—Lisa Richmond, *Seattle Office of Arts & Cultural Affairs*

↑Merrill

1953

WARREN AVE
↓MARY LYNN DAY

↓Ila Mae   ↓Mary Lynn   ↓Merrill

← Linda

PICNIC WITH THE KIDS
FROM SCHOOL & SIBS

←Ila Mae Morgan

WARREN AVE

Merrill on↗ end   WARREN AVE

Mom when Merrill
was a baby

↗ Merrill

Our whole family - Mom, Dad, Nina,
Sarah, Merrill, Linda (baby), Grandma,
Grandpa, 2 Aunts, 1 Uncle, 1 cousin

Introduction

"If you talk to someone, suddenly they might say,
"Oh I have a niece, or a brother, or cousin, or I have
a friend. Everyone has this experience but they don't
want to talk about it." —Delia Cano

Beginnings

My first meeting with the Seattle Family Network (SFN)
was a potluck. We went around the table and each
member of the SFN described their reasons for wanting
to tell the stories of the "senior families" in their community. These were parents who had raised children with
developmental disabilities during the post World War II
era. "We have stories—personal experiences that people don't know about—stories that at one time were
kept secret, but now people want to talk." The conversation was bewildering at first. Each person's reason for
wanting to tell these stories of the previous generation,
and their own personal story were intertwined. Every
member of the group at the table was a caregiver for a
family member with a significant cognitive disability. (1)
I learned that every family who has a child and/or an
adult with a developmental disability struggles daily with
complex issues. They must work to secure a variety of
social services, financial assistance, and appropriate
medical care. They advocate for meaningful educational
opportunities, recreation, jobs, and housing. They are
subject to whims in the economy and privately tremble
when new public officials are elected, not to mention
the variety of emotional and personal experiences they
must continuously work through. Yet they assured me
their lives were easy compared to the generation
before.

The World War II generation are often called the pioneering parent advocates. Invisible to most of us, they
rode a wave of social and human rights activism during
the postwar decades, activism that transformed life in
America. A quiet undercurrent of the civil rights movement, their first act was to challenge their doctors and
pediatricians by saying, "No, I will not institutionalize
my child." Nor would they abandon their children to the
jurisdiction of the medical/professional establishment.

When I was first offered the project, I wasn't sure it was
right for me. I'm interested in stories about the unrecog-
nized—how people struggle to realize a purposeful
existence in the face of considerable hardship. But disability, it seemed, was a painful story and with no end.
It also felt as if I was being hurled into the center of a
drama, where the emotions were so high I feared I
could never make sense of it. Yet the more I listened,

the more the experiences began to sound familiar. Six
months earlier my mother, who was 82 and diabetic,
had her second stroke. She had short– and long–term
memory impairment, problems with attention and con-
centrating. She was bewildered and angry. We were
told she could no longer live alone and were advised to
place her in a nursing home or an assisted living facility.
Though her story is about senior–care, the experiences
of my brother and I caring for her until her death in
2004 paralleled the stories in this project. We kept her
in her own home but agonized over finding the right
caregivers. We began a search for doctors, medica-
tions, and therapies. We pored over legal documents
about trusts, wills, and the multiple powers of attorney
one needs. We entered the labyrinth of insurance policies, Medicare, and the modern health care system.
We traveled regularly to the emergency room and struggled with personal care issues we were untrained for.
Every time we took her out shopping or to a restaurant,
I was surprised that even though the Americans with
Disabilities Act was passed in 1990 there were few
public places that felt comfortable for her to be in. The
world was too big, too busy, and there was almost
nowhere she could walk comfortably. My personal world,
as I tried to learn how to be a caregiver for my own
family member, began to mirror the stories in this project.

While my family experience would last but a few years,
the stories in *Becoming Citizens* were many decades
long and are still unfolding. As I spent that first afternoon with the SFN, listening and thinking, the scope of
the project began to emerge. This was a story of mothers and fathers optimistically starting new lives and families in a postwar economy with economic opportunities
they couldn't have imagined a decade before. Then a
child was born whose very existence, they were told,
would disrupt their chance for a better life. Unwilling
and unable to accept the idea that the child should be
given up—or that they should give up on this child—
they pushed forward. The conversation that day went
from anger to tears over funny and sometimes outra-
geous stories about home life and moms as bake-sale
activists. Mothers would describe baking cakes and
cookies to raise money for programs and schools, or
cooking fabulous meals to influence a senator about a
piece of disability legislation. I also realized that the
children who were kept out of the institution were my
age. They were my peers. But where were they? I don't
remember seeing them in grade school or high school.

Here were mothers turned activists over a cup of cof-
fee—the first moment they had to themselves after organizing a local playschool when their kids were denied

access to the public school system. Then 15 years later four of them would become leaders in a grassroots effort to enact a piece of federal legislation that would transform public education in America. This was a story both about missing children and the making of a grassroots movement that exploded nationally, passing significant legislation on education, housing, and social services, and contributing to the passage of the Americans with Disabilities Act in 1990. These were mothers and fathers as the unsuspecting designers of a new society for people with developmental disabilities.

We ate, talked, and laughed together, and many cried that afternoon of our first meeting. I soon learned that these were the emotions I should expect at the many meetings this project entailed. But just before we cleared the table and parted that day we identified four major ideas that became essential to the project.

1. We would interview and photograph at least ten families to tell the primary story of what families with a child with a developmental disability experienced between 1940 and 1980.

2. Within the stories we would chronicle the passage of the education law, first in Washington State, and then show how it and other actions all over the country led to the passage of the federal legislation. Within this chronicle we would also profile the four mother activists.

3. Built into the project would be the many reasons to capture these stories: so that they wouldn't be lost, to inform the local community about its history, to help young parents know that there is hope, and so that story-telling could heal the political divisions that over time had formed in the disability community.

4. To go public: to bring the private struggles of these families into public view would add them to the historical record.

Postcard of the Eastern Washington State Hospital, Medical Lake, no date

Historical Summary

While the primary focus of this book is on the ways parents struggled to keep their child in the family home, or the emergent parents' movement of the 1950s and '60s, historically the relationship of the family to the state institution is a complicated one. It's entangled with changing attitudes toward mental retardation as well as ideas about education, employment, civil rights, and citizenship, and is the foundation of these stories. It is a rich and complex history I can only briefly summarize.

In the 19th century

The history of disability is replete with stories of infanticide, child abandonment, neglect, and the placement of children in asylums and orphanages, yet there are also stories of children being loved and cared for in the family home and extended community. In the early 19th century, even though there were few schools, community records indicate that some children with disabilities went to the same schoolhouses that their brothers and sisters attended. Accounts from this era also suggest that if a child could contribute in some small productive way to the livelihood of the family, or at least not become an unnecessary burden, many lived their lives within communities. (2)

In 1839 the Jeffersonian ideal of public education found a form in the common school system championed by Horace Mann. It was believed that a nation composed of growing immigrant populations must be educated. Education was a way of socializing a mass populace, with citizenship as the intended outcome. During the 1840s the industrializing economy was erratic, and newcomers often had difficulty surviving. Families might break apart in a desperate search for work.

Almshouses, prisons, and orphanages grew as people struggled in cycles of poverty and employment. (3) Ignorance was considered a crime and poverty a form of deviancy. Operating in an atmosphere of uncertainty, attitudes toward mental retardation or "idiocy" also began to shift. Religious morality coupled with a pre-Darwinian concept of biological inheritance determined that the sins and social tendencies of parents were to blame for a child's disability. (4)

In 1847 Samuel Gridley Howe, an associate of Horace Mann, received state funding to, "inquire into the condition of the idiots of the commonwealth, to ascertain their numbers and whether anything can be done on their behalf." (5) His report cited an alarming growth in their numbers as well as the suggestion that the family home might be an unfavorable environment if they were to be helped. He also wrote that the children could be "improved" through specially designed educational methods. By the following year the first school for the "feebleminded" opened in Massachusetts. The school utilized the theories of Eduard Seguin and Jean Etienne Esquirol, who believed that "idiot" children could learn through a program of moral treatment and physiological education. (6)

By 1850 both the common (public) school and the state school for feebleminded children were established in Massachusetts, with subsidies from state and local governments. They shared the same goals—to prepare children to be educated citizens. One principle difference between the two systems was that children with disabilities, it was believed, could only advance in a residential school away from the influence of their families. In this setting they would be provided a "homelike" situation where they would be taught verbal skills, hygiene, and the rudiments of some useful skills so they could be returned to the community. While some did "graduate" from the "idiot" schools there was no support system for them once they returned to their communities. In the strained economy during and after the Civil War, many were sent back to the residential schools, or found themselves in worse conditions in asylums and prisons. (7)

Within the next decades the "idiot" school became primarily custodial. Less emphasis was placed on education for a life outside the institution. Although initially the schools were near urban centers, where parents might visit, many eventually moved to country settings, away from society, family, and public attention. Attitudes toward disability also changed. By the early 20th century, humanitarian ideas of educational improvement programs were replaced by eugenical ideas of contain-

ment. People with mental retardation were thought to be hereditary deviants, as having incurable illnesses, as being sexually promiscuous and dangerous to society. Sequestered in state and private facilities they were intermittently studied by doctors, psychiatrists, educators, and eugenicists. They became victims—of sterilization programs, training or work regimens, abuse, or profound neglect. While some schools maintained a level of funding that enabled programs and staff support, many operated under an economic and philosophical void. (8)

In the 20th century

Most of the early experimentation and theorizing about mental retardation and education occurred in the eastern United States, but with territorial expansion in the late 19th century the practices moved west. In 1886 a bill was introduced in the territory of Washington establishing the first school for "defective youth" in Vancouver. In 1889 Washington became a state and the following year enacted a compulsory education bill for "defective youth." This bill required parents to register any child with a disability, and send him or her to school. The legislation, although irregularly enforced, channeled children to the state institutions. In 1907 a second state school for the "feebleminded" was opened near the Eastern State Hospital for the Insane, near Spokane. (9)

In 1935, a group of parents in Washington State formed the Children's Benevolent League (CBL). These were parents whose children were under the care of the State Custodial School at Medical Lake near Spokane. As concerned parents they hoped to maintain contact with their children and contribute toys, books, and other materials to the school. They also helped one another cope with the difficulties of separation from their children. The parent members of the CBL were critical of declining conditions at the school during the Depression and successfully lobbied for funds to open Rainier School at Buckley—paid for in part by funds through the Works Progress Administration (WPA). The new school was also closer to Seattle and Tacoma, where many parents lived. CBL, a forerunner of the Washington ARC, successfully helped to create legislation over the next decades for expanded institutional care, but with more parental involvement.

For children with disabilities who lived with their families, special education programs were available in some public schools in the 1930s, but there were no clear guidelines for admitting children or excluding them. The administrators used the special education programs to funnel children to the state institutions. By the 1950s the state/institutional system was overcrowded and there were waiting lists for admission. There were also reports—from all over the country—of inhumane treatment and deteriorating facilities in state institutions. By 1968, in Washington State, there were over four thousand children with disabilities being served in five state schools. Because of these combined conditions parents in the 1950s and '60s began searching for new programs and educational models. Those parents who refused to admit their children to the state institutions and began creating alternative programs in the community were often at odds with parents of institutionalized children, about the best care for a child with a disability. They also often found themselves competing for the same sources of funding. (10)

Throughout the country during the 19th and 20th centuries, advocates for children with developmental disabilities have predominantly been parents. Although at times attitudes about disabilities have led to separations of parent and child, ideas began to shift radically after World War II and in some ways to echo an earlier era. Many parents believed strongly that their children should grow up in the family home. They began to reject the advice of the "authoritative professional," and they came to insist that their children should have the same opportunities non-disabled children enjoyed. The normalization movement popularized by Wolf Wolfensberger in the mid 1960s, as well as the Kennedy family's public admission that they were a family with a disability, gave parents new hope and an ideology. To parents, normalization meant, not that their children would be changed and made "normal," but that society would change and learn to accept, include, and appreciate their kids for who they were.

The Education for All Handicapped Children Act of 1975 not only provides a public education for every child with a disability in his or her community, it has had a profound influence on the decline of the state institutional system. Many parents could have their children at home and attending school in their local communities—as some described it, "Our children have at last somewhere they can be."

Building a Narrative – January 2002-2004

The project did not originate from a research question, but from spending time with a community. I live in San Francisco, so I traveled to Seattle every two or three months. I stayed in the homes of the members of the SFN and participated in many events and gatherings. We went to advocacy meetings and family circles and met with various professionals, from social workers to administrators in the field of disability. I visited group homes and was given a tour of Fircrest, a state facility in Seattle for people with developmental disabilities, which opened in 1959. We had community potlucks and we organized a history work group. We also conducted preliminary interviews and developed a working prototype of stories for people to discuss and critique.

The families selected were pre-interviewed by the SFN. We chose families with a range of personal experiences. Though some people preferred privacy, harboring old fears that harm or ridicule might come to them should their story be made public, most were very willing to participate. We also asked that they gather photographs, mementos, and any other materials from their personal collections that they thought might help us understand their family life. Stories often do not have convenient beginnings or endings, so the meetings were conversations rather than formal interviews. Often the family, or in many cases it was the mother we spoke with, had something she had been thinking about—conversations began to flow the minute we entered the home. We developed the following question "areas," or territories of conversation.

How did you learn of your child's disability and what did you do?

I wanted to learn the scope of the family's experiences, how they felt and how they made the decision to keep their child at home, even though in most cases they were advised to place the child in a state or private facility. Many parents were told their child's prospects were dismal. They were told the child would not learn or develop and that this child would also disrupt the possibility for a normal family life—the disability would adversely affect their other children and themselves. Most describe being bewildered. It became evident that knowledge about developmental disabilities was haphazard.

The parents characterized the doctors as having little experience and the profession as a whole as having no "procedures" in place for helping them. Yet many of the recollections also included at least one doctor or nurse

Collage by Katie Dolan made from news fragments in 1950. 1950 Baby Crop Means Big Business, Seattle Post Intelligencer, July 26, p. 5B; photograph by John M. Miller

who honestly said, "We don't really know how your child will progress—each child is different." Parents were given contradictory information and many were also advised to bring the child home and treat him/her like their other children. Their stories convey a sense of confusion and isolation. For almost every mother interviewed, retelling the story of how she was told of her child's disability was a profound reexperience of it. While some families chose to keep their child on the basis of religious conviction or fear of "institutions," most describe an almost gut sense that a life in the family home could somehow make a difference.

Two families in the project initially kept their child at home, but the severity of the child's disability and specific family circumstances influenced them to search for different options. In both cases they were advised to place their child at Fircrest though there was a period of time on a "wait list." Once the children were admitted, many family members maintained contact with their child, and the mothers of both children placed at Fircrest joined the parent advocacy group, Friends of Fircrest.

I asked them to describe the particular form of the child's developmental disability. The conditions include

Down Syndrome, Cerebral palsy, autism, epilepsy, and conditions caused by oxygen deprivation at birth, fevers, flu, spinal meningitis, and sometimes the causes were not known. While this book does not center on the reasons for the disability, or how it occured, every story provides some description by the parent, although knowledge was scant and often unavailable. While some parents embarked on their own research, others went from doctor to doctor, or searched for schools or special medical care. For most, and eventually all, the condition itself became irrelevant. Parents chose to concentrate their efforts on what they could do for the child socially. They searched for ways they could provide a "meaningful" life. They learned to see that child as a person and not as a disability. For many parents this was a pivotal moment, both in their home life and for getting involved in political actions.

What was your family life like?

The families describe how there were almost no services or programs to help them learn how to care for their "mentally retarded child." Some parents found an encouraging doctor, and some mention being visited in the home by social service workers. But most often they described how other family members, neighbors, and acquaintances helped them cope and find answers to their questions. Two mothers describe how a relative got them to recognize the disability and the task at hand. Another mother described an appointment with a neurologist, who said to her, "If you don't toilet train this child…," prompting her to realize what no other professional had even suggested: that it was possible for her daughter to learn. Most describe learning from within their own home-life context—with many of the family members participating in caring for the child with a disability as well as taking on extra responsibilities in the household.

While most people presented the positive experiences in the home there were also descriptions of feelings of shame and distancing from the child with a disability. Some describe strains on the marriage, fears of society, and psychological stress. One family member described how the family never expressed love for one another— all their love was focused on his brother. While some families turned inward, others, in reaction to so little information and so few services, started their own networks, organizing mothers groups to help new families prepare for the years ahead. Eventually many parents joined the Washington Association for Retarded Citizens (ARC) and/or other local and national disability organizations—their participation helped to form the national networks.

Describe your child's personality.

Every person with a disability in this project was born before 1965. Most are in their forties and early fifties.Of the now thirteen adults I was able to include the voices of all who were comfortable with spoken language. In almost every family interview they were present. I asked every family what special things they did as a family because of the interests of the child with a disability. How did they communicate with the child? Did they develop special ways of communicating? I attempted to create an existential picture of the person from within the family context. In many family descriptions the child with a disability was at the very center of family life— literally wedged between the other children in the snapshots of family events. Many times the family members described how important the experience of their sibling was to their way of thinking about life. In fact, some siblings grew up to work in the fields of disability and social work. In three of the stories the person with a disability had died in adulthood.

What educational opportunities were available to your child?

All the parents described the lack of educational opportunities and the ways their children were discriminated against. Many parents described almost a quest in their search for meaningful programs. I wondered what the parents learned about the ways their child learned. Often they described how the other children in the family coached their brother or sister. I was curious about the intuitive educational processes that parents may have tried. Almost all described the ways their children were smarter than anyone had led them to believe. Some searched for classes, special teachers or trainers, or reached out to other mothers and started community playgroups. I asked what social experiences the family had in the neighborhood or with the local institutions. Did they bring their children to public schools? If so what happened? For many, this became the key issue that motivated them—exclusion from schools, churches, community groups, and social services.

Were you involved in advocacy or political actions?

I asked the parents to describe how lack of meaningful programs drove them to start their own schools and parent groups and eventually advocate for educational rights. How did the parents get involved with a community of people who were concerned with disability issues? What did they consider activism? Did they think of themselves as activists? Would they have been involved in "political" work if their child did not have a disability? How did they go from unsuspecting parent to parent advocate? Every story describes some form of advocacy work and the various ways parents described their activism, from baking cakes and forming mother's guilds to writing letters to congressmen and attending demonstrations at the state capitol. Many also described themselves as nonpolitical. One mother said, when asked this question, "I guess I had to have a reason to be an activist." While it was not the intention of this project to study feminism and activism, it was another story lurking below the surface. Many of the "mothers" had defense related jobs during the war years, or had traveled across the country to secure jobs or an education. During the 1950s many women became homemakers, oftentimes reluctantly. Although their frustration in dealing with a system that excluded their child and the child's welfare motivated them, many mothers said they also identified with and felt encouraged by the women's movement. Many parents also identified strongly with the civil rights movement. Some expressed a feeling of optimism after World War II, which encouraged them to try and to make things happen for all their children.

Reflections on the past and future visions.

Every parent was asked to reflect on whether the world today is a different place for people with disabilities—and to envision the future. While most agreed that advances had been made in education, housing, and public attitudes toward disability, almost all had apprehensions for the future. They fear a change in attitude, which might affect public policy and funding for much needed community services and facilities. Their experience has taught them that when the economy suffers the first programs to be cut are those for people with disabilities. They all described their struggle as ongoing.

Family background

I asked each family where they were from and how long they had lived in Seattle. I was interested in the parents' professional backgrounds and their awareness of their economic prospects in the 1950s and '60s. I also asked how the parents had met and what, if any, wartime experiences they had. Over half of the families migrated from elsewhere, choosing the Northwest because of economic opportunity. Almost all of the parents met and married during the war years or just after. Disability cuts across class and economic boundaries, so the entire group represents a range of economic and social backgrounds. To allow the stories to flow and center on the disability experience, I included information on the family background selectively in the text of the story and alluded to it in the selection of photographs.

The Book's Organization

All the family interviews meandered through the same question areas, although the book is organized into five sections. Each section emphasizes a separate theme.

"About Children" presents the family situation. It is organized chronologically, with the first child in the book being born in 1936. It concentrates on how the families came to know of their child's disability, how they coped, and the choices they made. The stories also chronicle the child's life experience. This section also includes two families who placed their child in institutional care and the circumstances that led them to the decision. The individuals interviewed are Marcella Nelson and her daughters Linda Nelson and Nina Seaberg, Katie Dolan, Mary and Susan Saffioles, Helen Pym, and Joan Werner.

"About Schools" concentrates on the ways parents became motivated to search for and create educational programs for their children. It also gives a picture of the ways the parents went from isolation to grass-roots activism. Janet Taggart and Evelyn Chapman are two of the four mothers who authored Education for All. Mary Hiramatsu was a teacher in one of the first parent-run schools. Robert Bass was a civil rights advocate and school principal who championed desegregation for both Black Americans and handicapped children. Nadean Bass was an educator and active in the Seattle Mother's Guilds.

"Education for All" chronicles the passage of the 1971 Washington State law that served as a precursor to the federal Education for All Handicapped Children Act in 1975 (IDEA, 1990). It describes how Cecile Lindquist, Evelyn Chapman, Janet Taggart, and Katie Dolan emerged from a grassroots national movement of parents advocating for their children's rights. They describe how they built their connections in the community, how they learned to strategize, research, write, and utilize each of their unique skills to author and lobby successfully for a piece of legislation. It also includes reflections by disability lawyer William Dussault—enlisted to work on the committee when he was a law student—on the history of discrimination against people with disabilities in America.

"About Citizens" concentrates on adults with disabilities—where they live, their jobs, how they function in everyday life, and their prospects for the future. In this section the parents and family members reflect upon the many achievements for people with disabilities of the past 50 years—in education, work, housing, transportation, and personal achievement. They also reflect on the growth of the disability movement and the work yet to be done. The individuals interviewed are Vivian and Marie Strausbaugh, Doreen and Lance Peake, Myrtle, Bob, and Sherry McNary, and Dorothy, Dwight, and Sharon Gowdey. The family stories end with Sharon Gowdey reflecting on her life, work, and future.

The timeline enfolding the body of the book is a visual contemplation of the connectedness of official and unofficial histories. It is a conceptual visualization of the historical process. It sets experienced history—imagery developed during a community/history workshop—within a web of historical events, philosophies, and political movements. It suggests the entangled nature of history and everyday life. It also encourages the idea that the disability experience is a core element of the ongoing struggle for liberty and citizenship.

Visual Documents/The Family Archive

The story, and politics, of this community begin in the very space of domestic life. Families were interviewed in their homes. Each chapter is a braided narrative combining recollections of individual experience, photographs, and selections from the family's private collection of snapshots, articles, letters, institutional documents, and mementos. Families were invited to share any piece of "personal history" they thought relevant to retell the story of life with a child with a disability. Often I was given a tour of the home from the perspective of where photos were placed on the wall, in a hallway or room, or taped to a refrigerator. Family collections come in interesting packages: paper bags, shoe boxes, albums, drawers—they were pulled from closets, garages, attics, or directly from the wall or dresser where they were being displayed. Sometimes they were organized and labeled, mostly they were not. Many times materials were sent to me later and often I was invited to return when an article or album was discovered that "might help me." While I combined my investigations with readings on many related topics including the history of disability, disability studies, and education, this document's "presentation" concentrates on the materials and recollections the families provided me. I am interested in the ways every household is a repository of past experiences—an "informal" archive of past and present intermingled. I was also interested in ways I might elevate this informal method of retrieving information—directly from the domestic space where it was enacted—and reassemble it as a flow of historical knowledge.

While human memory is fraught with inaccuracy, distortion and subjectivity, many of the details within each individual's telling were reinforced through the collection as a whole. (11) Facts, fictions, knowing and not-knowing, hope and regret are the strange material of everyday life. Pieces of the story were told in different ways. Sometimes images reinforced a person's description, but more often images and words seem to conjure up or suggest a way of understanding that neither could have done alone. Images and texts were considered equally as pieces of information—sometimes intended to provoke one another. While the book is "constructed," the selection process was guided by listening to the story over and over until essential and disparate threads could be woven together.

Citizens

Through these stories I saw a matrix of ideas flooding society during the past century. While the social contract philosophers (Rousseau and Locke) first articulated the theoretical underpinnings of modern democracy—in their writings on equality, education, and human rights—in the 18th century, the ideas became fiercely public in America during the civil rights movement. Ideals of human equality penetrated daily life and influenced many tangential but equally vibrant social movements. Non-feminist mothers often cited an awareness that the women's movement helped make them able to speak out. What was due to Black Americans—equal education rights for their children—should translate for children with disabilities. People were subtly infused with a spirit of civil disobedience from the civil rights, antiwar, labor, and environmental movements.

Becoming Citizens is a set of stories in the struggle for disability rights in America. It is also a study of ordinary life and the multiple expressions of citizenship. It was born from conversations and an attempt to unravel the ways ideas turn into action: how a private experience can first isolate and then galvanize people, bringing their shared experiences into public view. It is about how unsuspecting individuals can be motivated to achieve the remarkable then slip back into oblivion. The project is not an analysis, but a "landscape of experiences" where the story streams of disability, education, politics, and the dream of civil rights flow together. Also embodied in these family narratives and photographs is an image of the "normalization movement," an emergent paradigm of the 1960s, which places the person with disabilities into the mainstream of daily life, requiring all of us to rethink our ideas of the "normal." (12) The citizens of the title are the persons with disability, their parents and family members turned political activists—and all of us who must learn to live in the world co-existing with people of differing capabilities, cultures, and politics.

Notes

1. Disability activists and theorists in disability studies have initiated a thought-provoking dialogue challenging the language and definitions used to describe people with disabilities or differing capabilities. The label used to describe any individual in society influences how one is seen and treated. Establishing respectful names for groups of people has become a highly charged and politicized aspect of contemporary life. I use the term "cognitive disability" or "intellectual disability" occasionally to remind readers that the people in this book have a disability where their thinking processes have been affected. The phrase developmental disability has a specific definition within the field. (Please see glossary.) Throughout this book, the contemporary phrase "people (or child or person) with disabilities" is used when talking about people today, however mental retardation is used in historical references. Many of the parents, in the 1950s and '60s used the conventional phrase of their times—"mental retardation" and still converse informally using this term. In the introductory sections of the book the currently agreed-upon phrase, person with a developmental disability, is used, while in the heart of the family stories the informal phrasing of mental retardation remains. For a compelling discussion on the use of language in disability politics see, Simi Linton, *Claiming Disability: Knowledge and Identity* (New York: New York University Press, 1998) pp. 8–33

2. In an article by Penny L. Richards, she writes that according to popular records in the early 19th century often children with disabilities were integrated into family life. She also cites examples of the ways children might learn useful skills and participate with chores in the home. Richards argues for a more thorough excavation of "vernacular" histories. On the history of mental retardation she writes, "An emphasis on the professional—on policies and theories and, on institutions and their practices—has left the personal and private, and the popular unexplored." See Penny L. Richards, "Beside Her Sat Her Idiot Child," Stephen Noll and James Trent eds., *Mental Retardation in America: A Historical Reader* (New York: New York University Press, 2004) pp. 65–84

3. Immigrants, people with disabilities, the insane, and the poor were often grouped together and feared during times of economic instability. Phil Ferguson, in an article on almshouses in the 19th century, points out that social welfare programs and their tangential institutions—almshouses, orphanages, prisons, asylums, and hospitals—are an integral thread in the study of disability in the 19th century and their relationship to emergent capitalism. Philip M. Ferguson, "The Legacy of the Almshouse," Stephen Noll and James Trent, eds., *Mental Retardation in America: A Historical Reader* (New York: New York University Press, 2004) pp. 40–64. Also see Irving Goffman, *Asylums: Essays on the Social Situation of Mental Patients and other Inmates* (New York: Anchor/Doubleday Books, 1961); and Michel Foucault, *Madness and Civilization: A History of Insanity in the Age of Reason* (New York: Random House, 1965).

4. Many of the assertions that parents could not appropriately care for, or were to blame for their child's disability were brought on by the temperance movement of the 19th century. Inadequacies of the individual were thought to be the root of social problems. Early in the 19th century theories about an individual's social ranking were determined by the mixing of religious morality and biological inheritance. Later in the century they were generated by the intertwining of social theory—Herbert Spencer/social darwinism and Francis Galton/eugenics—with biological theory—Charles Darwin/evolution. See James Trent, *Inventing the Feeble Mind: A History of Mental Retardation in America* (Berkeley: University of California Press, 1994); Wolf Wolfensberger, *The Origin and Nature of Our Institutional Models* (Syracuse: Human Policy Press, 1975).

5. Samuel Gridley Howe, "Report made to the Legislature of Massachusetts, 1848," reprinted in James Trent, *Inventing the Feeble Mind: A History of Mental Retardation in America* (Berkeley: University of California Press, 1994) pp. 23–26.

6. It was during the French Revolution that "enlightened" doctors first began to investigate the behavior and treatment of patients who were considered "lunatics" or "idiots" and were confined to prison/hospitals. Philip Pinel is sited as the first doctor to notice that the behavior of the inmates of the Bicetré prison of Paris could be influenced by exercise, light, and good food—or humane treatment. The "prisoners" he discovered responded to these treatments—their health improved and often they stopped behaving like madmen or criminals. Pinel was both a mathematician and doctor who had studied Rousseau. It was in 1793 during the revolution that he first unchained his "patients." Some he wrote had been shackled in their cells for 30 years. Eduard Seguin was a student of Pinel and like Pinel was influenced by the writings of Rousseau, Locke, and Condillac—on the nature of man and society, and the role of education. While these early educators/doctors had differing opinions about whether or not "idiot" children could learn, they were the first to explore the possibilities. For a theoretical discussion on the ideas of Philip Pinel see Michel Foucault, *Madness and Civilization: A History of Insanity in the Age of Reason* (New York: Random House, 1965). For an interesting discussion on the educational ideas of Eduard Seguin, see James Trent, *Inventing the Feeble Mind: A History of Mental Retardation in America* (Berkeley: University of California Press, 1994) pp. 40–59.

7. Sarah Mondale and Sarah B. Patton, *School: The Story of American Public Education* (Boston, Beacon Press, 2001); James Trent, *Inventing the Feeble Mind: A History of Mental Retardation in America* (Berkeley: University of California Press, 1994).

8. For a more thorough description of the change in attitude toward mental retardation in the late 19th century, and the remarkable transformation in thinking of the early education "humanitarians," see James Trent, *Inventing the Feeble Mind: A History of Mental Retardation in America* (Berkeley, University of California Press, 1994). For a description of the ways these philosophical shifts manifested themselves in the design of care, the architecture, and ultimately their embodiment in the state institutional system, see Wolf Wolfensberger, *The Origin and Nature of Our Institutional Models* (Syracuse: Human Policy Press, 1975). Also see Irving Goffman, *Asylums: Essays on the Social Situation of Mental Patients and Other Inmates* (New York: Anchor/Doubleday Books, 1961).

9. The compulsory education bill for feeble-minded children was repealed in 1957. Even though it was irregularly enforced, the Washington State Archive has long lists of children with disabilities from that era. In the early 20th century people with disabilities were stigmatized and eugenic sterilization laws were enforced in Washington State to control the spread of the "feebleminded." Parents often hid their children at home, or relinquished them to the state institutions. Numerous investigations of state facilities between 1880 to well into the 1960s found them under-staffed and overcrowded—often with people being abused and living in subhuman conditions. Wolf Wolfensberger, *The Origin and Nature of Our Institutional Models* (Syracuse: Human Policy Press, 1975). See also Burton Blatt and Fred Kaplan, *Christmas in Purgatory: A Photographic Essay on Mental Retardation* (Syracuse: Human Policy Press, 1975, originally published in 1966);

and Barbara Brecheen, *Developmental Disablilties Services: An Historical Outline 1861-1980* (Olympia: Publication of the Division of Developmental Disablilties).

10. For a history of the Washington ARC and their early advocacy activities see Larry A. Jones and Phyllis A. Barnes, *Doing Justice: A History of the Association for Retarded Citizens of Washington* (Olympia: ARC of Washington, 1987); and Larry A. Jones, Phyllis A. Barnes, and Russell Hollander, "Our Brothers' Keepers: The Story of Human Services in Washington," 1853-1937." *Columbia* Spring 1989.

11. I made no accurate count of the materials I looked through, though I estimate over 2,000 pieces of visual information—photos, snapshots, articles, and other documents. I have over 40 hours of interviews—800 pages of transcriptions, documentation and notes.

12. Normalization was an idea first articulated by Scandinavian activists Gunnar and Rosemary Dybwad. Wolf Wolfensberger, in his influential book, *The Principle of Normalization* (Toronto: National Institute on Retardation, 1972), promoted de-institutionalization and normalization—bringing people out of the state institutions and into the mainstream of daily life. This idea became a guidepost for many parents during the '60s and '70s.

Becoming Citizens

Family Life and the Politics of Disability

You're one birth away
from my experience,
that's what I think...

—Nancy Melzer

About Children

Sadness, grief, guilt and isolation are feelings parents described when they were told their child was "mentally retarded." The strange names for the diagnosis—mongolism, infantile schizophrenia, brain damage, spastic—were unknown to them. They turned to their doctors, pediatricians, and religious leaders for help only to learn that they too knew very little. Information was scant, contradictory, and often inaccurate. Based on "disreputable" research, mothers were often blamed for their child's "condition." The "prescription" most parents were given was to institutionalize. To forget about this child and have another.

Parents describe how dependent they were on the medical system for guidance. After nearly twenty years of hardship during the Depression and World War II many Americans learned to depend upon "official leadership" and agency programs for relief. Yet when they sought an institution for their child, they found that lack of funds and staffing during the Depression and war years left them overcrowded, understaffed, and with inhumane conditions. During the economic optimism of cold war America, to put one's child on a waiting list for the purgatory of institutional life, as it was often described, added another layer of stress, guilt, and anger. The relationship of the parent to the institution is the first chapter in this story and the first step toward civil activism for many.

"About Children" follows five families whose range of experiences gives a picture of the ways parents pulled inward, made choices, and grappled with issues in the home and community. While many kept their child at home, others chose an institution or special boarding school, though without abandoning their child. These parents stayed close to their child, visiting often and providing an ever-watchful eye. Their presence helped to transform institutional conditions.

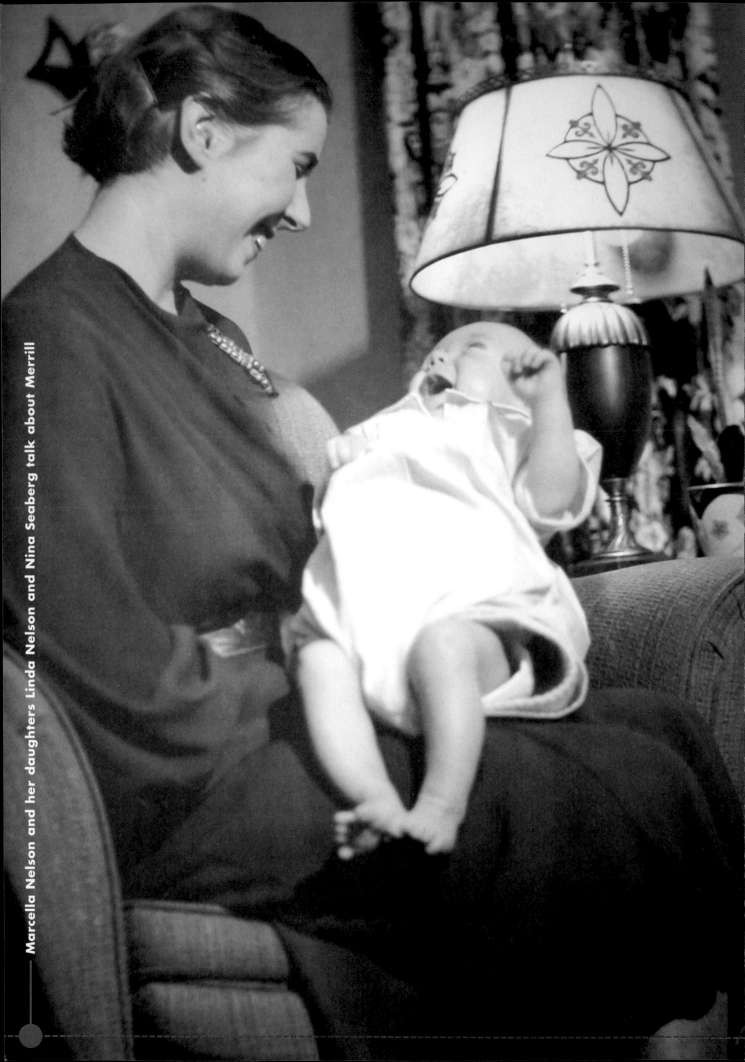

Marcella Nelson and her daughters Linda Nelson and Nina Seaberg talk about Merrill

The Nelsons

Marcella: Merrill was perfectly normal when he was born. When he was two days old, he got a high temperature and jaundice. It was the high temperature that caused the brain damage. It was 1936 and they didn't know how to treat him. The doctor just told me to bring him home and love him. At first, it was hard for me to realize that something was wrong. It was my husband's mother who made me face it. He was a good baby, but he was slower than my daughters. Then we found Dr. Wyckoff. They really didn't have any treatment; they called it spastic at that time. He invited Dr. Earl Carlson from New York, who had cerebral palsy, to meet with some of the doctors and parents and explain certain things to us, to make us aware of what we had to face. One doctor said, "There is nothing out there for your kids. If you want something to happen, you're going to have to do it for yourself." Another doctor suggested massage and to give him experiences. They said not to spoil him, he has enough problems. He was quite pysically disabled, and they said he wouldn't walk. But he did when he was ten.

Dr. Wyckoff was an orthopedic surgeon, and, unlike the other doctors, he got us to try and think of what we could do. A small group of us whose children were patients of his interviewed other doctors and got the names of their patients who had cerebral palsy. We were to find others and share what we knew. Some mothers were scared, some weren't, some were eager, others kind of held back, some were embarassed and ashamed. We were the mothers and others.

? WARREN AVE ? ? ? - I'm not sure where this is .   ↓Merril

↑merrill

I guess I had to have a reason to be an activist.

Children from the spastic children's school, c.1945, unknown location

We parents became really obnoxious after awhile. There was no special education at that time, and the public schools wouldn't take our kids because they thought they weren't educable. So in 1942, our church let us use their Sunday school rooms during the week. There were only six or eight children to start. There was a steep flight of stairs. I'll never forget those Far West Cab drivers who would come and help us carry our kids up those steps. I remember some of the mothers bringing their kids on the streetcar. So often they arrived late, or not at all. Miss Boxeth and her sister came to teach. They were older, but they taught speech and anything they could. Two old retired teachers—we convinced the school board to give us the teachers and pay their salaries. We had to cook for the school and clean. We charged $20, but we never turned anyone away. We had to prove that these children could learn. The teacher reported to the school board and we kept pressuring. I went to women's guilds to speak and Dad went to talk to legislators in Olympia. In 1944, there were so many parents blowing their horns they gave us a portable unit behind an elementary school on Warren Avenue and we became a part of the Seattle Public Schools.

Nina: My mother forgets. But I remember how upset she got when people called and said we have a neighbor with a child, we think it's in the back room, we've never seen it. Maybe this is someone you should contact, and of course, she would. Because of Merrill there were a lot of things we didn't do. But it was also World War II with gas rationing, and all kinds of things you couldn't do. But this was my family—it made no difference. Merrill was my brother. I don't think we were really aware that we were doing anything different. But we were the only kids who went to kindergarten with housemaid knees from scrubbing floors at home. But I thought this is just what happened.

Woman Named For Community, Church Work

Mrs. John M. Nelson, chosen for the honor because of her many contributions to her church, her community and her family, yesterday was named Christian Mother of the Year at Gethsemane Lutheran Church.

Mrs. Nelson's efforts led to the founding of the King County Chapter of the United Cerebral Palsy organization. A school for cerebral palsy victims was begun at Gethsemane Lutheran because of her determination to help children afflicted with the condition.

HER INTERESTS have taken her into many fields, the Gethsemane Church Women's executive committee, which picked her for the honor, said. Recently she became a founder of the auxiliary to the American Institute of Electrical Engineers, for instance, and is now hostess chairman for the group.

Her husband, John Nelson, is assistant superintendent of Seattle City Light. She is the mother of four children and the grandmother of eight.

Seattle Post-Intelligencer, May 8, 1960, p. 7

It's funny, I've always got the feeling

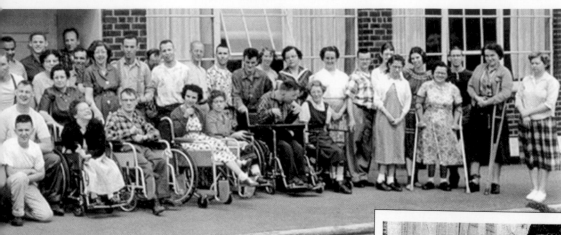

United Cerebral Palsy sheltered workshop, 1959

Linda: Merrill took a lot of Mom and Dad's time away from the family. As the youngest I'm aware that my sisters took care of me a lot. My mom and dad were always working on things. After Merrill graduated they hit the pavement and got a sheltered workshop started. After all the work getting him into school, they didn't want him home with nothing to do.

I think we were well accepted in our neighborhood. I do remember discrimination—going to restaurants where I was asked not to bring my brother back. There was always pain outside of our immediate circle of people.

Nina: One incident I will always remember is one day when we went with mother to a deli downtown. There was a man ahead of us in line—and mother said he was spastic. He couldn't talk very clearly and the waitress skipped over him. My mother said to her, "Don't take my order, this man was first!" We were young and shocked at her anger.

Linda: They always said Merrill wouldn't do a lot of things, but he did. He tried to talk, but you couldn't understand him. He would spell on the palm of your hand. He wrote notes and he used the typewriter. He was also an artist and did many paintings, and he read. When he got older he got angry because the story he wanted for his life and the story he was forced to have were very different ones. Mom and Dad made a point to give him as normal a social life as possible because this was a time when kids like Merrill would have been put in an institution—parents who had a child like Merrill would have been asked to sterilize him. Eugenics was popular at the time. We weren't just a family, we were a family with a disability; it defined our history, it defined our story. Merrill was my brother.

Honored Mother And Family

MRS. JOHN M. NELSON, named Christian Mother of the Year at Gethsemane Lutheran Church yesterday, is seen here with two of her daughters, Linda, 19, (standing) and Mrs. J. F. Stilwell Jr., 24, Portland, Ore., (seated on edge of davenport) son, Merrill, 23, and three grandchildren. Mrs. Nelson holds Jeffrey, seven weeks. Seated on the floor at the Nelson home, 5556-35th Ave. N. E., are Mark Stilwell, four, (left) and brother Stevie, six.   —(Post-Intelligencer Photo.)

Seattle Post-Intelligencer, May 8, 1960, p. 7

that people would say when they saw me, There goes Marcella, all

Marcella: When Merrill stood straight he was six feet tall. The opinion was that he had a high IQ. He read but I'm not sure how much he really understood. He was interested in his father's job with Seattle City Light. Our concern was that we would have to live forever—to outlive Merrill. Some of the parents started to die so we worked to get a residential home built. He met his girlfriend, Cynthia Fischer, there and he would have liked to been married, but he died before that ever played itself out. He died in 1991 from the same thing that caused his condition. He had surgery for his neck and they gave him a procedure to see if he could swallow. Well fluid got into his lungs and he died.

9

she talks about is . . . .

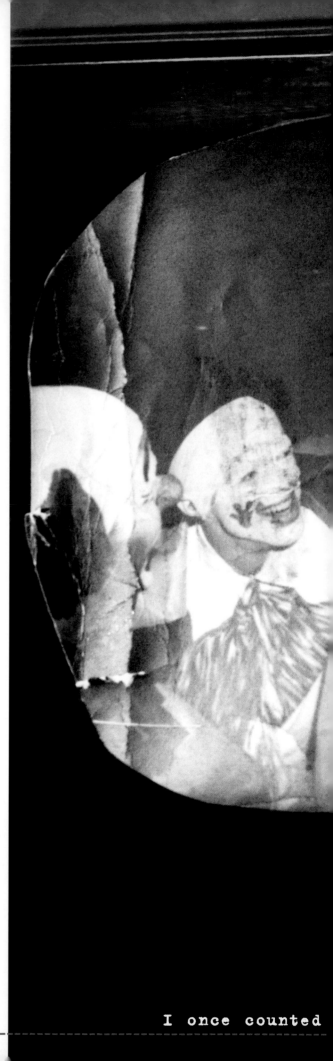

The Dolans

Katie: Patrick was born in 1950. He was my first child. The family literally worshiped this child. With autism you don't notice anything. Often they are beautiful children. He talked before he was a year old—all kinds of words. We thought he was so advanced. He didn't crawl; he walked and ran and climbed. He was three when he was diagnosed as infantile schizophrenic. Without any real tests or proof, they jumped to the conclusion it was the mother that caused it. We believed it. We grew up with the belief in God, Jesus, and the doctor—rolled into one. I mean if they told us to cut off Patrick's head and adjust a few things and sew it back on we would have let them. So I went into psychotherapy. I suppose it helped me. But it didn't help Patrick. He had stopped eating and talking. He'd walk up the stairway and throw himself over the door and kick the door back and forth. The doctors were stunned. I was afraid because I saw they were afraid. He was so wild and hyperactive and they couldn't get eye contact. A doctor back east finally diagnosed his autism. They said there was a school in California, but it was very expensive and Patrick was only three, we weren't going to send him away. They also suggested another school in Philadelphia, but I would have had to move there and my husband's business is in Seattle. I didn't see how we could manage. He was seven when we sent him to the school in Santa Barbara and twelve when he returned to Seattle. We weren't able to send him until my father died and my mother gave us a little money to help for the first year's tuition. It was a school for millionaires and movie star's kids. They dressed them up in white shirts. But he began having violent seizures. They really couldn't handle him and they didn't seem very scientific. So we moved him to a school for children with developmental disabilities.

that I saw over 100 doctors. We got many different diagnoses:

Patrick often had good teachers, but he was so unpredictable. They would tell me. "He's not 'mentally retarded,'" but he's different than the other children. One elderly woman, a speech therapist, called me all excited because Patrick said, "Humpty Dumpty had a great fall." They sent me telegrams and everything. He was ten or eleven but he never said it again. That was in 1961. The woman nearly had a nervous breakdown and she quit. One day he would pick up a pencil and draw a perfect sailboat and they didn't even know he could hold a pencil. But he'd never do it again; it kind of disallowed their professionalism. Children with autism will do those kinds of things. We understand it now—but they didn't

when he was a child. Then he started having violent seizures—nonconvulsive epilepsy and temporal lobe seizures. He'd run and scream and throw himself against walls—they couldn't handle it. We learned of a treatment center in Washington. We had to assure the doctor we would move there so Patrick would be admitted. I had six or seven jobs. I had to earn money. I worked as a model and did commercials. We didn't move, but we drove him 180 miles a day for three years and carpooled with other parents.

Eventually he was kicked out. His behavior was too extreme. I brought him back to Seattle. And because of my TV career—I had a local show at the time—the head of special ed at the school district, whose wife just loved my show, finally admitted Patrick to Pacific School. After a few months he was kicked out. Patrick was fifteen when we took him to Northwest Center. The criteria were he had to be toilet trained and recognize his own name. They also told me if he could point to something he wanted and recognize it he could learn to read. That day at the grocery store we looked at a calendar and I asked Patrick to show me the dog and he did.

I got excited; someone was going to teach him to read. Ten days later they called me. I could hear him screaming in the background. They told me he was never to come back. I picked him up and as I drove him home, I mean I was pregnant, but I contemplated driving off the bridge. I'd taken him everywhere. I had nowhere to go. My doctor feared for my new baby and we even took Patrick to Fircrest, where they turned him down. I heard there was a program at the Seattle Parks Department and they were accepting kids like Patrick who had behavior problems. Then my new baby died of sudden infant death syndrome. I had good

counseling. I also went into a yoga class where they had us go into a deep trance state and I couldn't come out of it. They had to call to me and convince me I was not giving up on someone who had died. I came out of it but I finally realized that the child I was grieving for wasn't the baby—it was the child I lost when Patrick was diagnosed. It was his life that I had never accepted. I finally saw him as Patrick Dolan and not as the person I wanted him to be—to dress up in clothes and behave certain ways. I was always trying to find a doctor or school or a way to cure him. It was then that I got involved with the Parks Department and Evelyn Chapman and Janet Taggart to make changes, not in our kids, but in the very system itself.

receptive aphasic, uneducable, untestable, untreatable, untrainable.

We mothers developed fantastic cooking skills and could put a potluck together in an hour at any time because we couldn't go anywhere else. You didn't go out in big family outings, because often your own family rejected you. They didn't want you to bring "him" along. Of course restaurants didn't want our kids either. So you got together with other parents of handicapped children and had pot luck suppers. This was our social life. It was the '60s and women started speaking out. Women in those days were treated like they were "mentally retarded." But mothers across the country who didn't have programs for their children with disabilities were starting their own. They ran them, furnished them, and they found volunteers to teach. I mean these mothers were tough and they got organized. Rather than struggle every day to keep our children in programs we began to look at legislation that could help. We wanted our children to have a chance.

Patrick knew more than we realized. In this photo of him with the record—we didn't know he did this for years. He takes 33 rpm records and plays them at 45 speed. He moves the needle across listening to that chipmunk voice and he finds phrases. Once he had Perry Como singing "Seattle, Seattle, Seattle" until the needle went through the record. But I can ask him things and he'll pick out a phrase from a Beatles song or something and play it to me.

Once my friend Janet said to me, "Did you ever notice,

Once he spit a mouthful of water in the face of a doctor. Another "expert" doctor we went to see, Patrick faked like he was falling asleep, I know he was thinking, "I'm not going to listen to this crap." This doctor, like so many others, couldn't help him. We took him to a lecture once, and it went on and on. He made it obvious he wanted to leave, but I said no. He knew how to get out of any public place, he would just openly masturbate—and we got him out of there fast!

There are so many things they understand about autism today. A child can almost be normalized by the time they're five. Patrick didn't get a chance.

Today Patrick lives with an attending family in a house he owns and he has a job. They are a wonderful family who understand and care for many of Patrick's needs. He's the grand Patriarch. He is perceptive and develops relationships with people. But I'm a little embarrassed to say, he wants them with people who are non-disabled. All the work I do now is for young families who are facing a life with a family member with a disability. I don't want them to go through what we did. Our work is prideful of people with disabilities. But I understand Patrick because who would want to be associated with only one group of people—that's what normalization and being in the world is all about.

Patrick treats you like you're mentally retarded?"

Mary Safioles and her daughter Susan talk about Stella

Stella Safiole

Switch Activated Tube V rat

Big Green Switch

Vibrating Pillow

Tape Player/ Tapes

Place item on Stella's lap tray; if she
pushes it away offer her another choice.
Stella enjoys rocking in her rocking chair.

I went down to 109 pounds.
Mentally I couldn't take it
anymore. But I held on to
the idea of a better house
and found a realtor.

Susan: And that realtor picked
Stella up and he would carry
her—we had a broomstick and he had a convertible. We had the broom stick-
ing out and Stella in the back seat and my mom and sister in the front . . .

Mary: And that's how we entered the neighborhood. But my marriage
became more stressful. I didn't think I'd last. With five kids welfare was out
of the question. They all had godparents but no one could take care of Stella.
I had no other family so I filled out the registration forms. It took five years
before she was admitted. In 1963 there were over 700 people living at
Fircrest. Now there is only about 200. It was terribly hard for her at first to
be confined. In the beginning they would put the residents on a big area
on the floor and they would crawl and some of them would bite. Then they
would be put in cribs and they'd stay there. But what could I do?

Susan: It was more like a warehouse then—and there were abuses. Stella
would wring her hands, which my mother interpreted as anxiety. Later in
the '60s things began to change. The attitude now is different—it's about
the individual and what they can learn to do.

Mary: They built new buildings and just last year one woman here could tell that Stella wanted to rock. So she found a rocking chair. It is the biggest thing of happiness Stella has had. It is a good staff; we are very happy with her care and hope they keep Fircrest open. They talk about budget cutbacks and we've called our congressman. I come here every week and my husband, too, would come. When he retired he took full care of her. I think a kind of guilt came over him. He did everything for her . . .

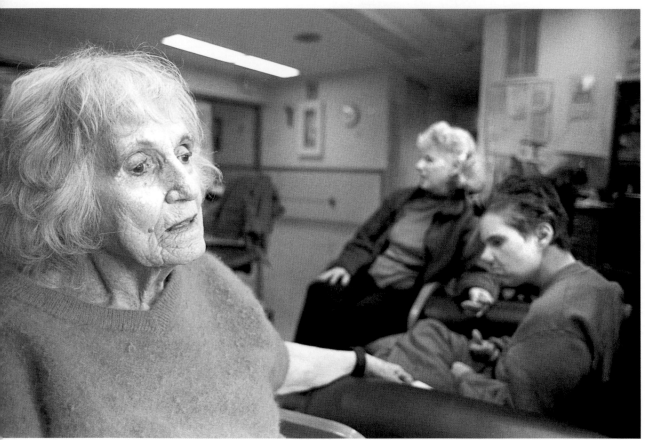

Mary, Susan and Stella at Fircrest, 2003

Susan: I think my parents are truly amazing. Usually the male can't handle it and there is a divorce. But just like my mom said, after my dad retired he put all his energy into Stella. So that speaks well of him even though I know they had a rocky time. Of course, my mom is steadfast. She didn't go into an emotional abyss, which most mothers probably would have. She kept her family together.

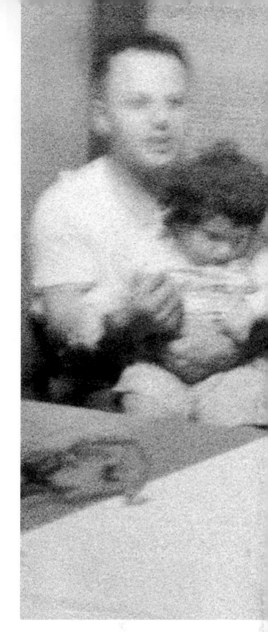

She had a walker and then she had one of these big round seats with a tray in front and she would roll around the house in that. She would scoot. She scooted all over. In fact we bought another house suitable for five children and Stella's room was upstairs. She'd come down the stairs and through the dining room—and through the stairs outside. In the summer she would go out those doors and down the steps. I never worried about her. She would get on the davenport and bounce. She was very active. But the seizures got worse and there were times we had to take her to the emergency room for convulsions. There was a sulfa drug that helped, but it had side effects like kidney damage and other things. They stopped giving it to her and she went down from there.

Susan: When we were young we would all sing "Old Macdonald Had a Farm." Stella was very little—five years old—and she sang too. She loved music and she had some words she could say then. We didn't think anything different about her—this was our reality.

Mary: My Husband and I had problems. He had a good job managing a shop but he was down on the world. We had a small house and my oldest daughter slept in the attic. His attitude was that we had a roof over our heads, what else could we want. He didn't think we were worth it. He rejected our friends. He worked long hours and many nights he'd stay out with his buddies. I'm not a great cook, but I always had dinner on the table.

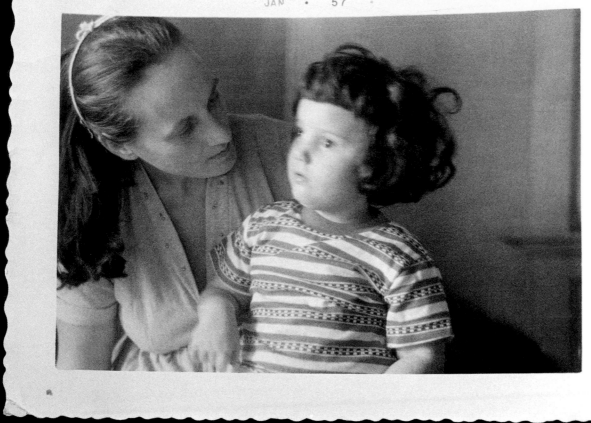

JAN • 57 •

The Safioleses

Mary: I think sometimes Stella has memories of home.
Just recently on the radio, they were playing Christmas carols.
She came to a stop. It wasn't a seizure; it was like a memory.
It was a happy time for Stella that's how I interpret it.

She was born in 1953. When she was nine months old she had
strep throat and it developed into spinal meningitis. She came
to live at Fircrest in 1963. She was ten. It was recommended
because I had five children. A women came out to visit us, she
was from the state community services. I wanted therapy for
Stella. She saw our situation and she advised us that an institution is what we should do. They advised we should place
her before she was five. It's sad because before they're five
that can make an adjustment that Stella never could.

never intended to give her up, never, we didn't think that way.

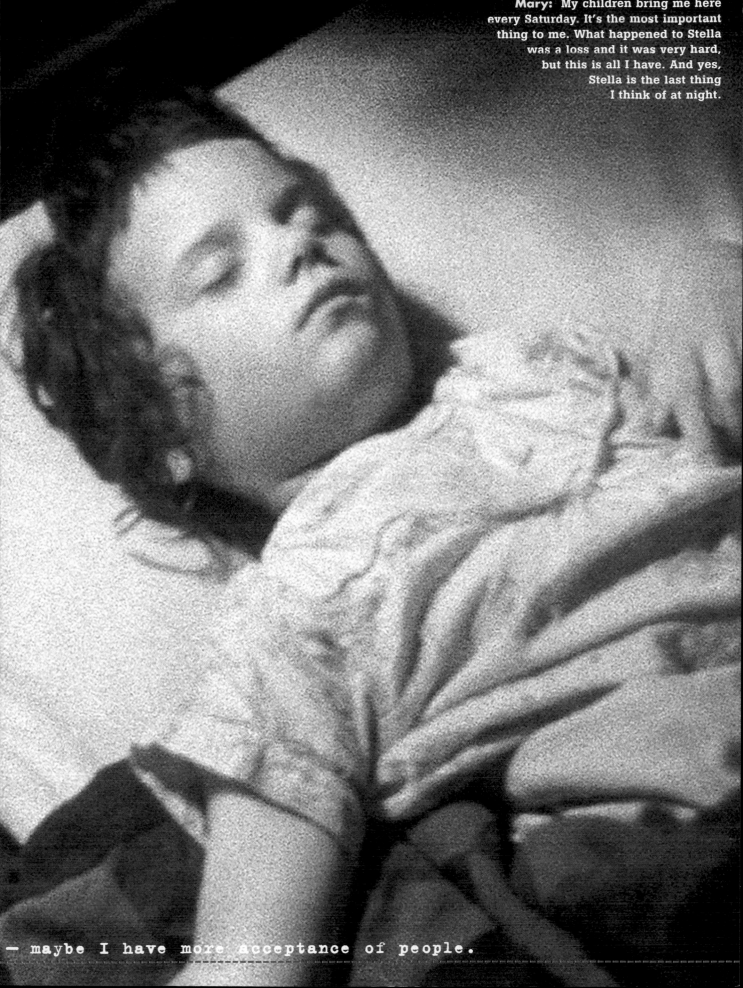

Mary: My children bring me here every Saturday. It's the most important thing to me. What happened to Stella was a loss and it was very hard, but this is all I have. And yes, Stella is the last thing I think of at night.

— maybe I have more acceptance of people.

Helen: She was born in 1955, around midnight. The doctor talked to me for awhile—not about Martha, he just talked and left. The next morning he told me Martha was a Mongoloid. He said they tend to be happy children and sometimes they're the pet of the neighborhood. But you can put her in an institution and forget about her and have another baby. I'll never forget those words. I thought I can't tell my girls I didn't bring Martha home because something was wrong with her. I cried for three days, looked at myself and said, enough, lets get on with life. The best thing I could do for our family was to deal with it. My pediatrician said we have no idea how she'll get along, but that I should treat her like a normal child.

Helen Pym talks about Martha

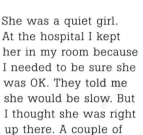

She was a quiet girl. At the hospital I kept her in my room because I needed to be sure she was OK. They told me she would be slow. But I thought she was right up there. A couple of times people would ask my neighbor, "Does Helen know Martha's retarded?" And of course I knew. It was good for her to be treated "normal," and if I ever babied her she'd let me know. Her sisters were wonderful at teaching her. They would make her say words over and over—they were taskmasters— but Martha learned to speak very well. My husband never could quite accept that he had a child that wasn't perfect. He always kept himself at a distance—afraid to get too close.

Martha was six before I ever encountered another parent who had a child with Down Syndrome. It was a program at Children's Hospital and there were parents of children with other disabilities too. Until then, my feelings about her problems were mine. It was a revelation to meet other parents.

I thought the school for Martha would be the Nellie Goodhew School for Handicapped Children. However, the school closed and the classes were put in the public school. They put a big cyclone fence all around the playground where the handicapped children played. They said it was so they wouldn't run out on the highway, but I think it was more than that. Naturally, her class was in the basement and all the restrooms were on the main floor. Many of these kids had difficulty with stairs. It was not quite integration, but it was something.

Then when Martha was in first grade the head of Special Ed for the school district put her into this craft type class. He said she shouldn't be in one of the adjustment classes because children with Down Syndrome can't learn to read. I said NO. I want her in the adjustment classes. I insisted, and he said it might damage her psyche, to be in competition with other children. I said I'd be prepared to take that responsibility. And of course, that's where she belonged—where she could learn. Within a year, it was this wonderful miracle she was reading.

When she finished high school we worked with Dr. Jerry Sells at the CDMRC. He taught a class to medical students about developmental disabilities. Martha described her experiences living in the community with a disability. She loved talking to them about what it was like growing up with Down Syndrome. They were amazed. She saw herself as a teacher, as if that was her purpose in life. Through the University she had several jobs but there often wasn't enough training. Someone with Down Syndrome must really understand the details of how to do something, and once they understand, they're fine. When they make mistakes, it's because they don't have all the information. Her trainer didn't get that. So she left and worked for one of the handicapped schools—working with children, she'd play games, she was very sweet with them. She was a volunteer, and she also worked with seniors.

Martha was always struggling to find where she belonged. After her father died, I began to worry that "mom" was her only security. We had a guild for retarded children—the guilds were always made up of women. Our kids were older, and we were worried about what would happen to them when we were gone. In 1968–69 the state was moving people out of institutions and into the community. The Group-Home Bill said they would give each person coming from the institution $400 a month. But of course it was the parents who had their kids at home who were starting the first group homes.

We worked out with the state that we would paper admit our kids to the institution, making them eligible for the funds. The actual amount finally was $200 a month, so of course we spent our time with bake sales and fundraising. It was the "normalization movement" and the influence of Wolf Wolfensberger, and the idea of de-institutionalization. I mean it's not normal to share your bedroom with a hundred other people. One of the parents was a builder, so he built the house. The state determined who lived there. Three from the institution and four from the community.

Martha was born 10 years too soon. Society wasn't ready for her.

She'll never progress beyond a ten year old,
she'll probably die in her teens.
This was the thinking. So the whole philosophy said,
Don't waste a lot of time on these kids.

Martha was twenty when she moved into her first group home. I tried several living situations for her. In one state-funded program she shared an apartment. One day when I asked how things were going Martha said, "OK, but I don't like this other person living with us." Her roommate had invited another rather troubled girl to move in with them. I called the staff, and this progressive guy said a young woman needed some help and that it was good for Martha and her roommate to help others. I said the state is paying for these two girls to live there— not to entertain someone else who needs help. I was the only parent involved so it took a lot of pressuring. They finally evicted her. But that same weekend she came back with her boyfriend and he raped Martha in her bed on Sunday morning; she still had a key. I brought Martha home.

Finally, I got her on a Section 8 housing rent subsidy. She got a rent subsidy and her own apartment. She did fine living by herself. She could cope with her own problems, but not with others. She wanted to run her own life, and she did well. There were problems, once someone complained about the smell of burning food and assumed it was Martha. The landlord checked, and it was another tenant. But whenever there was a problem the odd kid always got blamed.

Having a child with a disablitiy is a universal experience and I realized it the more I got to know other parents. We were young parents—in control of our lives. We'd organized things the way they were supposed to be. The baby is born, the baby is darling and then this happens. It's out of your control—there's nothing you can do. You ask for help, you want someone to talk to, you want to know how to care for this child better. At the ARC we talked about this. "Wouldn't it be great if we could help one another." They wrote a grant and I applied for the position. We called it the Parent to Parent Program. First we trained parents, and we worked with nurses and doctors in different hospital delivery rooms. We did better with the nurses. The doctors were suspicious of us. They were afraid of what we'd say to their patients. I mean the doctor drops the bombshell on the parents and then he runs. He doesn't want to see the bloodshed—and the nurse comes in and mops up. First we had to convince them to call us and we would help. We worked with the hospital staff and met with parents. We couldn't help everybody, but we gave them some comfort and ideas of what they could do. Even today people tell me what a help this program was to them. When I look at my whole life and the things I've done and accomplished, if someone were to ask me what seemed the most significant, I would have to say Martha. She gave me an extraordinary perspective on life and influenced my value system immeasurably.

She died of obesity—heart problems and sleep apnia. It wasn't a Down Syndrome problem, it was a self-image problem—dealing with life. After the rape and other scary things that happened to her in the community, she stayed home and ate chips and pizza. Short of locking her up, I couldn't do anything about her eating. She was living the quality of life that she wanted to live. She knew she shouldn't be eating those things. Her breathing got heavier; she didn't exercise. I knew her life would be shorter, but it happened sooner than I thought. She was thirty-seven. But it's important to me that she didn't die of Down Syndrome.

Martha was always protective of me. Even when she wasn't feeling well she would maintain that everything was great. I carry this photograph because it reminds me of her personality.

I've always been fond of this picture; she looks so "normal." There were many places we went, and people didn't know. In 1968 there was a checklist. If you had so many symptoms you had Down's. It wasn't until they had the genetic test that they knew. She was the typical 21st chromosome.

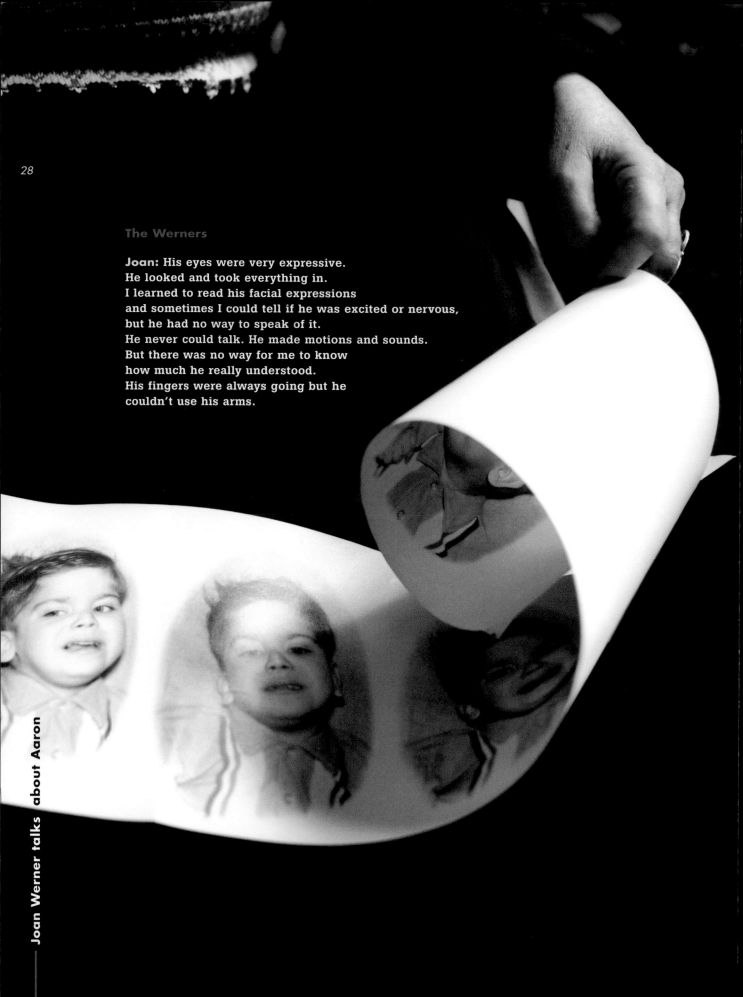

The Werners

Joan: His eyes were very expressive.
He looked and took everything in.
I learned to read his facial expressions
and sometimes I could tell if he was excited or nervous,
but he had no way to speak of it.
He never could talk. He made motions and sounds.
But there was no way for me to know
how much he really understood.
His fingers were always going but he
couldn't use his arms.

Joan Werner talks about Aaron

My family was very independent, I didn't know other

Joan: I have four boys and Aaron was the baby, the last one born in 1961. In 1961 the institutions were full. It was kind of a shock when I found out I was pregnant I hadn't been feeling too well and then I gave birth to him. My husband, who I'm no longer with, said he didn't look right. The doctor said he might be slow because he was kind of a preemie, but he didn't progress. He wasn't responding the natural way most children would. The doctor said we should place him in an institution because it was going to be worse than having a pet and it would be more difficult as time went on. But when we checked into that there were no facilities available to him. There was only limited space—and a waiting list.

We moved to a big house in Tacoma. The kids would carry him downstairs before they went to school and put him in the corner of the couch where I could change him and take care of him all day. I had back problems by then. The doctor told me to stop lifting him or I'd need surgery. So I would sit alongside him and with an arm sling slide him on to my lap because I loved to hold him; he was so good. You get so attached. I guess because they're helpless. It was really hard to part with him. I didn't get to go to school functions to see what the other kids did because I was homebound. I did my own projects. I painted, I made my own clothes and refinished furniture. Aaron was so dependent on me and yet some days when I felt lonely or blue, he'd be next to me and I would put my head in his lap and I would cry—and he would stroke my hair.

Our family gave all our love to my brother Aaron.

My husband went for his masters degree so when we couldn't place Aaron I said, "Lets take him with us!" We'll try to be as normal as we can." I mean he had seizures, but the whole family traveled together to Salt Lake City. We camped all the way. We had a nine-passenger country squire. My husband and I would sleep in the car and put Aaron at the head where I could see him all the time. We took hikes in the canyons and took turns checking on Aaron; we couldn't carry him. He was always easygoing and good natured.

We came back to Seattle, and after awhile we started going through changes. The kids were getting ready to leave home. It became a tug-of-war—too much for me to take care of Aaron and I couldn't stay at home all day any-more. I can't remember how long he was on the waiting list but he

had some seizures where we were advised to place him at Fircrest and I couldn't carry him any more. The pediatrician said I'd feel a lot better if I did it. I didn't like the idea. I didn't want to part with him really. But she told me they had adopted European methods of doing things. They had a cottage system. I felt better when I saw how it was and met the people who worked there. So my husband and I placed him at Fircrest in 1974. Four months later, we divorced. All I had ever known for the past twelve years was changing diapers and taking care of kids. I needed something else.

I took some courses at the community college and found a job at the university. I liked talking to people so it was a good job for me. I visited Aaron twice a week, and one of my sons did too. Mostly I think his care was good. But one time they started a new program—to push them to advance to their best potential. One day when I visited he was on a mat with another kid who was banging his head. They were alone in a room and I thought he could very well be banging his head on my son. I wanted to give it a chance, but I told them I didn't think this was right for him. He had already been bitten and then I found out that he had hepatitis B—I wondered if that was from the bite, or the medication, or what that was. I never knew. He always recognized me I think, but after awhile I couldn't visit as much. I'd had two hip operations and it was harder to get around. I think he got filled in with these other faces that fed him and took care of him and maybe he couldn't remember me as well.

I think our love for one another was sublimated.

They had been downsizing at Fircrest ever since we went. They always called me about things they did or changed. Once they had to rush him to emergency for aspiration of his food. He loved to eat but they had to put him on tube feeding, they were afraid. He was tube feeding for almost 5 years. They did that with a lot of the people there.

I guess someone else wanted the property at Fircrest. They did offer us another place for him to live but I felt better with him at Fircrest, I knew everybody, I knew the facilities, and there were places for me to park and I'm handicapped now too.

I used to drive over to see my mom at the nursing home and then over to see Aaron. One day I was at the shopping mall—in the restroom and a woman came in and hollered my name. I guess they were paging me. I knew it was either my mom or my son. She brought me to a security guard who gave me a phone number to call and that's when I found out.

Aaron died August 8, 2001. He was almost forty. He used to like to sit at the piano. And I guess he was sitting there and someone discovered that he was blue.

They put him down and started working on him, but it was too late. I kept calling the hospital because they were doing studies and blood tests, all kinds of things. I called them three or four times. "Well no," they said "We'll let you know when we have the results." They never called. But I noticed things before that. I would be talking to him and he would act like he was frightened, like something was going on inside of him. I asked the staff, but they said it was nothing.

Healthcare should be a priority in this country, when they downsize what do they cut? Healthcare. You can't do anything if you don't have good health. I once met another mother, a professor's wife—she was way up high. She had a wonderful house and she could afford an infirmary below, with their own salon and everything. I thought that was really nice—and if more people could afford to live like that. I came from a small town where everybody knew and looked out for one another. I miss the intimacy. Now everything is so commercial. Could it ever come to the point that if a family had a person with a disability in their home they could have the facilities to care for them? Maybe someday there will be a duplex where the doctor and nurse live next door.

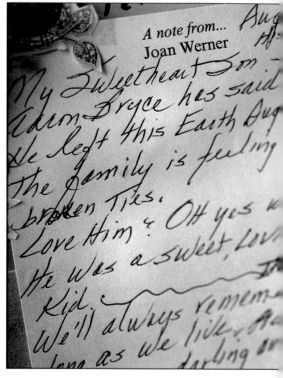

Some of the parents would
say, "My other kid goes to
school, why can't this one?"

—Janet Taggart

About Schools

"She can't sit in a chair," was the assessment given to five-year-old Naida Taggart when her mother Janet brought her to school in 1962. "Yes, I know," Janet said, "I want you to teach her." Even though she knew Naida had a severe form of epilepsy, Janet hoped her slow but growing abilities might be improved in school. Janet and Naida were sent home that day and told not to return.

Children with disabilities were randomly admitted to the public school system during the 1950s and '60s. Though many state constitutions provided wording guaranteeing a public education for every child in the state, schools and school districts had irregular policies. For children with a cognitive impairment, admittance was determined at the discretion of the principal or special education director. Many parents noticed that while in the home, surrounded by people—adults and children—their child did learn things, though often slower than their "unimpaired" children. It encouraged them to believe that more instruction, or special instruction, or maybe just being around other children could help their child progress.

In 1963 Janet Taggart placed an ad in a local newspaper; she was "looking for a playmate for her retarded daughter." A phone call connected her to a groundswell movement of mothers who were organizing schools and playgroups, hiring teachers, and developing programs for a generation of children virtually "locked out" of the public school system.

"About Schools" presents a selection of stories of how mothers and fathers began to build educational alternatives for their children, while learning to agitate for programs—entangling themselves in issues of civil rights and constitutional law.

The Taggarts

Janet: As parents we hung together or we had nothing, we were absolutely on our own and in many ways still are. We had a real talent for picking up people along the way, some followers, some leaders, but it all shook out.

Naida was born in 1957. She had little seizures all the time. We knew something was wrong. The pediatrician prescribed phenobarbital, the medicine of choice at the time. I was told she would never do anything, never walk, never talk, never sit up—a totally dismal diagnosis. I went to the library to try to understand better what I could do to help her. It was awful how ridiculous some of the suggestions were. One book said that children with "mental retardation" should be dressed in drab clothing—"Don't dress them in bright colors like red—it will draw attention to them." Well I didn't pay any attention to that, I mean she was so cute, of course I dressed her up in lots of nice things. When she got a little older we took her to a highly recommended neurologist and he said to me, "If you don't toilet train this child, I'll see that's she's taken from you." It was the best thing anyone could have said, because up until that moment I never thought she could learn to do anything. You see we had decided after her diagnosis that we would have no other life but to take care of this child. We had a boat in the basement and fishing and camping equipment. We gave it all away. It was symbolic. The neurologist wasn't brilliant, but he got me off my butt. I did toilet train her—in a week. She learned the same way any other child would. In essence, she was much smarter than anyone had diagnosed and could learn to do things.

Eventually I brought her to the neighborhood school and the principal and secretary literally escorted me out the door. I felt so isolated and it finally dawned on me. I mean I had no place to go and I assumed there was no one else in the world, so I thought if I put an ad in the paper perhaps somewhere, someplace I could reach someone. Ethyl Williams answered the ad. She had a daughter with Down Syndrome and they were just forming a playgroup. I went to the first meeting and that eventually led to Central School. It started in the basement of Temple De Hirsch.

I'm looking for companions or playmates for my daughter

The Rabbi had a child with a disability and when one of our mothers said to him, "Rabbi, I understand you have a disabled child." He answered, "Schoosh, don't say anything." It was an era when people hid these things. It's so sad. But he did let us use the rooms during the week. There were seven rooms. We had to move all of our school furniture out Friday night. We scrubbed and waxed the floors. On Monday we moved everything back in. We found some teachers. Most of them weren't certified, but they had some experience. Mary Hiramatsu and Naomi Murray were very skilled. One teacher worked with my daughter. Naida just frayed around. It was as if she didn't know where the beginning or end of things was. She had no sense of her environment. She was just sort of out of it. She didn't seem to recognize her limitations or who she was and where her world began and ended. Her teacher would roll her in a rug and hold her close, but keep her in the rug. Pretty soon Naida had a good sense of where she was. This teacher just figured it out. There were a lot of things these teachers could have taught "certified" teachers.

tle Post Intelligencer, Saturday Forum, 1973

F THE PEOPLE

who do have a right " with industry and making its opinions n to this committee of Con- gress.

MARK R. CASSIE
Spokane

Guilt Burdens

Parents of disabled children welcome the article which took issue with the practice of many non-medical people of labeling children as mentally ill without diagnosis . . .

The burden of guilt attributed to parents of disabled children is often placed there by the professional who implies that the very existence of their child is unhealthy for the family.

JANET TAGGART,
Seattle

P-I Forum

who's mentally retarded.

APRIL 1973

SUNDAY	MONDAY	TUESDAY	WEDNESDAY	THURSDAY	FRIDAY
1	**2** 3:30 Lowell School Auditorium. Teachers. Procedures funding. where we are now. SPEECH	**3** Call John McShane to tell him place of meeting. noon = N.W. Center- Advis Council	**4** QUARTER ENDS ~~12 p.m.~~ 1 PM Ch. 9. Arnliss Cecile is elsewhere 9:30 A.M. MR Board meeting	**5**	**6** AA Here
8 SUNDAY EASTER	**9** MONDAY MR 2:30 Emer. planning 7 p.m. mayors House 1:30 King T.V. 9:30 A.M. Bill signing in Olympia	**10** TUESDAY noon - 2 P.M. garden com cent Park garden PTA Noon - metro Demo. club	**11** WEDNESDAY Meet by Pacific School + Ryder - 11:30 Health neb - 3-5 n.w. center	**12** THURSDAY WCH WORKSHOP MUSEUM OF HIST. + INDUSTRY.	**13** comm Coali #104 Center
15 SUNDAY PALM SUNDAY ~~Monday~~ King-T.V. Spot	**16** MONDAY HOLY WEEK SPRING VACATION 9:30 - North West Center	**17** TUESDAY 7 p.m. Spec. Ed. Ad. Council	**18** WEDNESDAY 10 A.M. D.D. party 10:30 MH/MR Board 1:00 - MR. planning	**19** THURSDAY School 3-5 - Spec. Ed. Budget	**20** FR
22 SUNDAY EASTER SUNDAY	**23** MONDAY	MATRIX TABLE **24** TUESDAY U. of W. School of Nursing Eliz. worthy 2 p.m. 9 A.M. Seattle U. Campion Danm. Dining Room.	Health neb - 3pm **25** WEDNESDAY Election of neophone M. R. Advis Council Rep ~~Ruchana~~ ~~Speech~~ Cancelled	**26** THURSDAY Ellen Foscue = noon Aberdeen 8 p.m. - out 10 dinner. 6:30	**27** FR Of noon = Skipp 12:15 Joeta
29 SUNDAY 1:30 p.m. Mt. Zion Church w JANA - Rhinestone Club luncheon.	**30** MONDAY Babysit Cecile Noon = 9407 16" S.W. Grand opening	1:00 Slade Gorton	MARCH		

MARCH
S	M	T	W	T	F	S
					1	2	3
4	5	6	7	8	9	10
11	12	13	14	15	16	17
18	19	20	21	22	23	24
25	26	27	28	29	30	31

Foundation for Handicapped Children

4409 Interlake Avenue North Seattle, Washington 98103 (area code 206) ME 3-2003

7 SATURDAY

14 SATURDAY

21 SATURDAY
Allan's
BiRTHDAY.
PARTy.

28 SATURDAY

AY
W   T   F   S
2   3   4   5
9   10   11   12
16   17   18   19
23   24   25   26
30   31

So while our kids were at school we mothers had time to go next store to a little restaurant. It was the first time we had to talk. At first we exchanged stories about our kids. Did yours do this? What did your doctor say, and what did you do? That's how I learned and believe so much in putting parents together because you'll find solutions to problems. Getting parents together was both educational and volatile, because soon we began to talk about other things. First, we needed money and transportation. We wanted to pay the teachers. We all pitched in ten dollars a week but some couldn't afford it. We wanted support from the public schools. The only state money available were the Epton funds. It was overflow money. You had to put your child on a waiting list for an institution, but because they were so overcrowded the money you got could be used in the community. We hated doing this. I remember when I first came to Seattle after the war, on some days they'd let people onto the grounds of the state institutions and parade the "inmates" around like a freak show. We were against the institutions, but we convinced a lot of the parents to get on the list. It was the only way at first to support our programs. Kathryn Epton was a legislator, but more importantly she had a child with Cerebral palsy. In the back of our minds, we began to know that legislation was the only way we could get our kids anything. It was during this time that the political activism began. We tried to get support from the Washington ARC, but they didn't seem to understand. They were so used to abiding by the beauracracy of the public school system they couldn't comprehend the idea of transportation, much less educational support. But it also took us several years before we figured out exactly what we wanted and learned how to get a piece of legislation passed.

We were going all the time. There was such a long history of institutionalization that parents never had to thnk about programs. Now we had to start them, find teachers, and money. I just suddenly saw that it wasn't Naida alone any more, that all these kids had to go to school. This was a movement. We had it in our minds to go out in the world and create a space for these kids. It was very clear This was for everybody. By the time we got Northwest Center going there was a core of four of us: Katie Dolan, Evelyn Chapman, Cecile Lindquist, and me.

Phil: We were pretty exhausted most of the time. I helped by being the janitorial service. I took a cleaning contract with the temple—about twenty hours a week. The parents scrubbed the rooms, and at night we cleaned and vacuumed the temple and the Rabbi's office. I had a security patrol business too. We also had three adopted children.

Janet: Life was not comfortable for us. We had applied for adoption before Naida was born. Afterward, we didn't think we would adopt but they called and Ken came. He was eleven and he was great with Naida. He was with her the first time she stood up. Then Jana came. These were troubled kids, who were older and had nowhere to go.

Mamie: I asked to be adopted when I was thirteen. I was sent to good schools; they took me traveling. When Janet went to Olympia she'd take us kids and after the meetings we'd go to the county fair. I work now as Naida's support person while I get my nursing degree.

Janet: The state pays Mamie. The bulk of the available state and federal monies goes to the institutions, because it costs a lot to maintain people. Parents who chose institutions had no other choice. You want the safest possible environment for people with disabilities. There is money dedicated for community services and it's cheaper to maintain a person in the community than in an institution. Slowly the institutions are shrinking and the services in them have definitely improved. The parents who stuck with their children even after institutionalizing them reformed the system by demanding quality care. Unfortunately though there is often political hostility between us as we struggle to find the best possible support for our children. Historically we have been divided. It wasn't easy in the beginning caring for Naida at home. We also depended upon Fircrest for respite care. The whole family was involved at home. All of us mothers had supportive husbands. We couldn't have done this if we didn't.

Phil: I always knew Janet would be active—she completed her English degree after we were married. She was a great writer and a speaker. We worked constantly and when they got the mandatory education law passed—well there was a climax to that and it was worth it. When I look back I wish that—well, if Naida had had speech therapy, if she'd been in a program, she'd be able to speak. The form of epilepsy she has cut off the part of her brain that controls speech. She once did have a word or two. She says "atta" for dad.

Benefits of handica

By Mrs. Janet Taggart
Education for All Committee

For years, public education has limited itself to providing education for those children they judged best qualified to receive it. To qualify, children could not have any limbs missing. They must not be blind or deaf. Above all, they must not behave "differently" or appear to lack any of the mental capabilities found in the "normal" child.

Unfortunately, the Catholic Church has been caught in this dilemma. It was unable to provide the costly programs necessary for the uniquely handicapped members of their dioceses. It couldn't possibly provide one classroom for a blind or deaf child. Facilities were just not available. Neither were the wide diversity of programs necessary for each type of handicap. Meanwhile, Catholic parents of handicapped children continued to pay taxes and assume the burden of educating the privileged only. No wonder, after years of frustration and sorrow and heartbreak, many of these parents banded together to demand that the state live up to its constitution by providing education for all.

Needless to say, the state has been brought reluctantly into serving our neglected children. Those on the side of the bureaucrats, however, who rigidly fight change of any kind, continue to cry out. In their subtle way, these opponents pretend they are speaking for parents of handicapped children while, at the same time, they are doing everything possible at all levels to continue to deprive handicapped children of a proper education. These are the same forces who cried out not too long ago that handicappped children, particularly those with limited mental capabilities, were not "educable". However, with many of the children now becoming tax-paying citizens and no longer a burden on society but contributing members, the credibility of these chronic complainers has grown weaker and weaker. In desperation, they now resort to misrepresent the provisions of the law.

This civil rights legislation, known as the Education for All law, guarantees the right of all children to an education. This includes the blind, the deaf, the physically and mentally handicapped — those beloved children of thousands of parents across the state. This law came into existence through the loving and dedicated efforts of these deeply - concerned mothers and fathers.

This civil rights law not only guarantees the right of all children to education, but parent rights are also protected. This includes participation by parents in the process of determining which program is appropriate for their children. It also provides the legal means for them to sue individuals or groups whose service they (the parents) judge to be inadequate or inappropriate.

Specifically, the new law provides the following:

(1.) That all handicapped children shall have the opportunity for an appropriate education at public expense as guaranteed them by the state constitution.

(2.) That transportation be provided for those children who are not ambulatory and for those who are incapable of protecting their own welfare while traveling to and from school.

(3.) That school districts unable to provide appropriate programs may contract (a) with a locally approved agency or (b) a neighboring district. For example, some small districts have only one or two multiple-handicapped children for whom very sophisticated facilities and skills are

Catholic Northwest Progress, 1973

Janet: I honestly believe that everyone should have a fair crack at everything that's available and that it's the government's responsibility to protect people who are vulnerable. These were some things that my father taught me. He was a socialist who became a New Deal Democrat. We lived in upper Michigan, a hotbed of activism. I remember vividly before World War II started my father said they are killing people in Europe. Hitler is killing people and nobody is doing anything. He was very, very upset by this and I remember feeling really awful, awful that I couldn't do something. It seemed to tear him apart. My father had a great influence in helping me decide what's important in this world.

pped bill defined

required. (Transportation is provided for children attending either agency or neighboring district programs. Furthermore, a recent local special education policy insists that children spend no more than one hour on the bus either way).

The law further requires:

(1.) That lack of physical facilities does not release a school district from obligation to provide a program. Any facility which meets state code requirements may be contracted for this purpose. Children who must remain at home because of severe impairment (or children temporarily home or hospitalized) can receive itinerant tutoring services.

(2.) That laws governing non attendance and consequences are the same as those operating for regular students in regular classrooms.

(3.) That sanctions against districts not complying with the new law include withholding nor more than 75 per cent nor less than 25 per cent of all state funds given to that district.

The parents of handicapped children in the state of Washington could have gone the route of parents in Pennsylvania who simply sued the state for denial of their children's rights — and won. Unfortunately, the burden placed upon that state was immediate and devastating. However, Washington parents, mindful of these consequences, chose to take action in an orderly and legally - sound manner. They called for a survey of children not presently served by the state educational system. A line item in the governor's budget was requested and granted. This paid for the cost of educating many of these newly-found students during the two-year implementation period now past.

As of July 1, this law has gone into effect. Parents of handicapped children, after years of bitter disappointment and endless struggle now see that their efforts have not been in vain. There is hope now for their loved ones.

"Forbid them not," He said, "for of such is the Kingdom of Heaven."

Janet: Naida is forty-five; she was twelve when the education law was passed and then she could attend public school. I think the thing that drove me was the rejection. If you dig deep with every parent it is this horrible fear of rejection and the sense of isolation that follows. Wherever I went Naida was rejected—from school, from church. The first day she went to public school I was so afraid they might call I didn't answer my phone. Finally I did, and sure enough it was the principal. He said to me, "Listen, when you send Naida's lunch could you wrap it in wax paper? She can't get the sandwich out of the plastic." He ha, I'll never forget it . . .

1957

Mike Heiramatsu   First Schooling
    Margaret Johnson
              died Jan 1998
  BF Day basement
Larry Heppell
Clark Kitazuko
Sammy Sokolick
Bobby
John Wolgemuth   Frank Blanco
Naomi Murray — Mike's second teacher Central Y

My class

na Weighall ! ?

Mrs. Hirama

Rex   CENTRAL
Bucky   SCHOOL

           Denes   Robert
           Deahl   Atkinson   Elizabet
                         Larry
                         Heppell
           ✗
   Charlotte,
   Gatermaye's   @ Temple De H
   mom   & Kathleen

The Hiramatsus

Mary: There were playgroups spread out all over the city. These were started for kids who were handicapped in some manner. The first playgroup Mikey went to was in the basement at B. F. Day. Margaret Johnson was the teacher. I don't remember how I knew about it. I used to catch the bus, a very long bus ride. Mikey was three but he wasn't walking yet. It was way across town. We had free time waiting for everyone to come. After a while, the mothers and children would arrive and we had circle time where we would all sing together. I helped out every day. It was too much for me to go back and forth. I did whatever I could; the fingerpainting area or getting the snack foods ready, or clearing up after active time. Pretty soon I was working there. I thought that I might have inside knowledge, since I had one of these children right in my house. I could learn from him and teach the others. Later I got a scholarship and went to Seattle University and studied the Montessori method. I don't think I would have gone on to be a teacher if it hadn't been for Mikey.

I wouldn't have been a teacher without Mikey.

Eventually Mikey and I went to Central School, it was just across the street from us. Soon we found family-life coordinators that helped find teachers. The classes were in one large room in the basement of the temple. I always had a camera in my classroom. The parents stayed and sat next to their kids to get them to do the movements to the songs. That was one of my beliefs. The best way to get the kids was through the songs that they enjoyed with move-ment, they like the action. "Hello Larry, how are you? How are you? Hello Larry, how are you? And what will you do now?" I clapped my hands. We sang little songs where they could get involved with the rest of the group. "Open shut them, give a little clap. Open shut them, put them in your lap." "Spider" and all those little songs that they liked. That set the mood of the day. We'd do a little bit about whether it's rainy or cloudy or what day it is. What did you do on the weekend? We'd count the kids. I tried to teach them to write their names. Later I taught at Seguin School. It was a private school and the parents had money. We made a lot of the equipment that the kids used—sandpaper letters and numbers; we had them trace the let-ters and numbers on the board and in the air. We used all the senses to involve and stimulate them to learn to write. For these children, we needed to go beyond just saying it and naming it. We discovered, for some of them, it helped if they felt the movement.

There weren't any public school programs for our children. I often joined other mothers on trips to the Public School Administration building to try and get them to take our kids. Mikey was nine when he first went to a public school. The quality of teaching was very uneven at first. I think the schools were overwhelmed trying to figure out how to integrate the children. He used to be out in the halls a lot helping the janitor; the teachers let him do it. This was his first school experience. I think he got everybody wound around his finger. All he had to do was grin and get the broom and sweep the lunch room. He learned that early I guess.

I thought I could learn from him and teach the other kids.

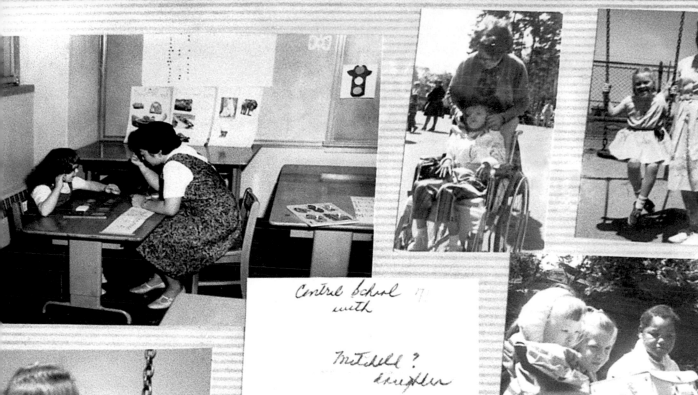

Central School
with

Mitchell ?
daughter

Woodlane Park/
Kay Herndon
molly H.
Harry Ann
Charlotte   Dania Scott
        Annette Gibson

Michael was born in 1954. It was a long delivery and his lung collapsed. The doctor said he would not be normal. His bones were brittle and somehow they broke his leg. I'm not sure how it happened. We didn't have to pay the bill. We were dumb and innocent I guess. Now people would sue. He has a syndrome. I can't remember what it's called, it's not Down's. We took him to Children's Orthopedic when he was nearly three. They said he'd be very slow. They gave him tests with block patterns. But at that age, I don't know how they can tell. He didn't walk till he was three. That was a major event—he went up the ladder of the slide at B. F. Day School. It was the first thing he did, he climbed up there and he shouted at everybody, to look at him. Then he came down. When I saw him up at the top of the slide that really encouraged me. "Well, he's going to go someplace," you know. That was the first playschool he went to. It was being around other kids. That had a lot to do with it. At home he learned things from his sisters, they wrestled around just like all kids.

It's hard to understand him when he talks. He puts things together very fast. When we're on the phone I have to say, "Mikey I can't see you," because he makes motions. We just did the best we could. His older sisters were a lot of help. They all played together and he learned things that way. Mikey likes to do things independently.

I really wanted him to have a job—just a small job, It didn't matter what it was. I just wanted him to be happy—he's happy when he can buy things. He once worked packing boxes. He liked driving the forklift. Today he lives in a group home, he's forty-eight. You know I remember that he liked to drive the tractor on my nephew's farm in Hawaii. Maybe he should have lived on a farm.

47

Evelyn: When my son Coolidge
turned five we were pulled into the
politics of special education.
In the Seattle Public School system
the Special Ed program had been
serving deaf and blind children for years.
They also served some children with
other kinds of disabilities
who were well behaved and
who knew how to sit still
and follow directions.
This wasn't Coolidge.
He was extremely hyperactive.

Evelyn Chapman talks about Coolidge and the search for programs

I had been surviving day by day with Coolidge. He was so hyperactive and he couldn't talk. We tried Ritalin for awhile, but it made him sleep all the time. Through the Seattle Parks Department where Coolidge went swimming, I learned of a new program. It was at Northwest Center for the Retarded and it was called the Specialized Training Program. It was for kids who had gotten rejected from the public schools. It was here we met Gerald Stinson and learned of behavior modification techniques. First, you establish tangible goals. The first goal was to sit still. Positive behavior was rewarded with M&M's. The so-called M&M economy was a classic form of reinforcement and it worked wonderfully with Coolidge. It's now laughed at, but I couldn't complain. Stinson would work with him one on one. It was intense, he would take his hand and sit him down and reward his behavior. This would go on all day for six hours. The parents saw results in kids they were told couldn't learn anything. This technique got kids in the right frame of mind for learning. Coolidge also received basic skills in reading and math and he started to speak more clearly and he was much better behaved at home—easier to live with. This program started a revolution. We learned that our children could learn, after years of being told they were not "educable." Parents were desperately trying to get their kids enrolled.

Coolidge entered the Seattle Public Schools after the Education for All Handicapped Children Act passed. He was twelve. His educational program included some academics and some "prevocational" training. By the time he was in high school he was also in a special education program but he still couldn't read very well. I was not happy. I met with the principal and the planning team and told them that "I want Coolidge to be able to read a newspaper when he graduates from high school!" Well they found this wonderful teacher and within a year he was reading, at a fifth grade level, but it was incredible. I also asked for special instruction in handwriting, because he could only print. I had to monitor the program all the time but looking back they did a pretty good job. I was unhappy with the vocational part of his education because they had very stereotypical ideas of what people with developmental disabilities can do. At the same time I enrolled in the Master's degree program in special education and early childhood at the University of Washington, and began to learn more about best practices in special education. It gave me some idea of what to ask for. I was also on the Special Ed advisory council. I got very plugged into what was happening.

All the kids in one way or another learned so much from being in school. Coolidge became very independent. It turns out he has the memory of an elephant. Someone taught him to ride the bus and that's his lifetime occupation. He knows every route and everyone along the way. He uses the Internet, he's gotten interested in photography. He still has difficulty talking, he has a kind of aphasia. Unfortunately, he's now rejected many of the programs that could help him. He doesn't see himself as handicapped. He's in the community, but he's lacking in social skills. These are the hardest things to learn and to teach. One might think you pick them up naturally—you learn how to be weird naturally. They need to learn basic social skills. This is really the basis for job retention and being included meaningfully into the community. I think all the girls need to be able to wear black dresses and pearls and talk at cocktail parties. The boys should, well, learn how to dance!

When Coolidge went to Northwest Center it was the first time I got to know parents with kids with all kinds of disabilities. I drove Coolidge to school every day. Kids in the public schools got bussed, but of course our kids never did. In many ways it was a bonus because that's how we got to know one another. Through Janet Taggart who had organized a speaker bureau for the ARC I met Cecile Lindquist and Katie Dolan. I also car-pooled with Myrtle McNary. At first we chatted about our kids, but soon we ran the Mother's Guild at Northwest Center.

couldn't avoid it.

There were about 80 of us. We organized an annual bazaar and ran many events together. At first we tried to get more revenue for the Park Department to run more handicapped programs, but we didn't really know how to do this. Katie and Janet had connections politically and a much better idea of how to pull off public relations events. It was Senator Fred Dore who inspired Katie to organize a Legislators Luncheon. We asked them to support quality special education programs.

We got our feet wet. Afterward a smaller group of us began to meet. We knew education was going to be one of our strongest priorities. There were four of us housewives—myself, Janet Taggart, Katie Dolan, and Cecile Lindquist. We recruited two law students to research special education laws in the country. We didn't precisely know what to ask for. But we started to talk more about education and what it meant and why it was so essential for our children. We didn't know it would be a civil rights law. What we now know as a civil right, or the right to an education really means that no child will be rejected, as ours had. We wanted a zero-reject policy. By this time too we realized that you couldn't just give your unformulated idea to the code-revisers office and get the legislation you need. Every word counts. We knew that we had to write the legislation ourselves. After many months of strategizing and lobbying, the Education for All Bill passed in May 1971, with full implementation in 1973.

I was an English major in college and have always had my nose in a book. I had no real career goals after college but I ended up a legal secretary for years. My father always told me never to join any organization. We lived through the McCarthy era and he was painfully aware of what happened to people during the cold war. I joined the young Republicans when I left college but more to meet people than for politics. I was apolitical really until I had Coolidge and then I couldn't avoid it. Being political has also brought our family life-long friends and allies—and a lot more work to do.

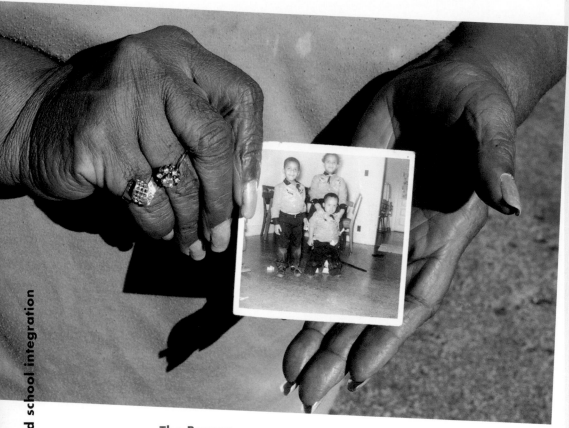

The Basses

Nadean: I knew immediately after his birth that something was different about David because of the way he looked; his eyes, his hands. I'd already had two other children, so it gave me the idea that something was wrong. But the way I really knew was by sending pictures to my brother-in-law who lived in Kansas. He said you can tell that he's a Down Syndrome person. As a parent, I was wondering why my doctor couldn't tell me. I was advised before I left the hospital. I can't remember who the person was, but they said that I should sign papers. All I can remember going on in my mind at that time is that if I signed anything it would be legal. So I didn't. Then we came home and we talked about it. What to do with David.

Robert: The first stage you go through—well, I had to get through my depression. I didn't want to talk to nobody, nobody. But after a certain point—let's go for it. Nadean's decision was significant for me. She said "I want my baby." That's where Nadean really got involved, because I'm trying to make a living for my family and Nadean's out there trying to find out what programs were available for my son.

Rosco: David was brought up in a regular environment, not in an institutional environment, a home environment. He participated in all of our family activities. We came together on holidays so he learned a lot of things that he would never have learned in an institution. He listened to our language, he saw the kind of games we played. He was a part of the family, he wasn't isolated, he wasn't kept away. He enjoyed the same experiences, from camping to boating to everything.

55

Nadean: As far as I knew there wasn't a lot out there for me. I didn't try to teach him anything—just to give him a lot of love. His back was weak, and I remember we had a swing that we put in the door. I used to tie him in there because he would fall over. I guess I accepted the fact that he could not learn. Whatever happened I was happy that it happened. I just began to talk with people and I found Central School. When he was three years old that's where we took him.

Robert: My brother Rosco and I took the children to the mountains. David was very young—six or seven. Some of the children were older, but they played, thowing rocks, they hiked and then they decided to wade in the stream which is very, very cold. It came right out of the mountains. I can always remember watching David. He wanted to go in that water too, and I didn't say anything, so he went in, but boy he came out in a hurry! Too cold for him, but he enjoyed doing what other kids were doing. We looked at movies. The kids drew with him, we played games with him. Nadean taught him how to chew. We did those kinds of things. Lots of birthday parties, lots of Christmas parties. Lots of getting together, just laughing and talking. He was one of the family. I don't think Mary and Bobby, David's brother and sister, had any early experiences different than David.

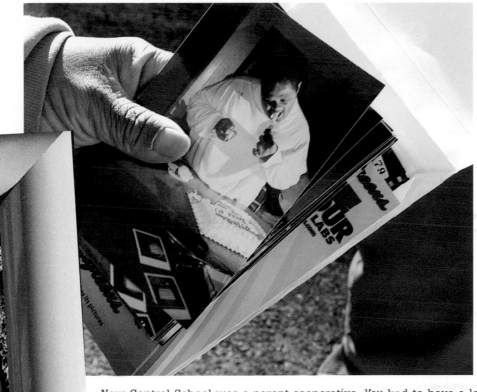

Now Central School was a parent cooperative. You had to have a lot of participation and Nadean had worked with Head Start. We went to that school because of Naomi Murray; she was an aide at the school and a friend. If you look at special education in the district, at that time they never admitted these kinds of children. They weren't toilet trained; they weren't this, they weren't that. Central School was a blessing. They taught them how to get dressed, pouring, really household daily-life skills. It took a while; not until these parent cooperatives merged did it begin to take a flavor in the public schools. We came together and we didn't have to pay the teachers. They got on the payroll of the Seattle School District. It made it really a lot easier, they provided transportation. Lets face it—Evelyn Chapman, Janet Taggart, Katie Dolan, you see they were real—you talk about aggressive.

Nadean: The thing that helped me at Central School was the parent meetings. At first you feel like you're all alone. I was just a mother who had a child like this. But we'd sit in a group and they'd introduce themselves. There were doctors and lawyers. I found out about all these people who were professional quote, quote, who had big money and big jobs—their experiences were quite different than mine. I still felt like I was better off. I met some Down Syndrome kids who were able to talk; they had verbal skills which my child did not. But some of the parents were unhappy with the child. It was kind of disgraceful to have this child at home. I'll never forget—we went to one parent meeting and there was this little girl and she could do everything; she could really talk. But they didn't want her in the home and the parents finally got rid of her. They institutionalized her, and she was quite capable, way better than my child. But it was the stigma of having a Down Syndrome child.

Robert: A person should be able to move as far as their capabilities. It's my role to facilitate activities for that child. My reward is when he's able to do a job and get back home and tell me he's accomplished something. He worked cleaning pots and pans and putting dishes away. I observed him. He knew where everything went and that transfers to the home. He'll tell me "Dirty, daddy" pointing to something in the kitchen. When I had my operation he was right there helping me get around. I mean, what he learns is for him, for his satisfaction. He has his own room, that's his place. We made provisions for David to have this house—

nonrevokable. My children will be his legal guardians. They can decide if they live with him, or if someone else lives here.

Nadean: We made a decision for David to stay in the home. I looked at group homes and I didn't like them. It was little things, the turnover of the supervisors and there weren't many Afro-Americans I saw. But it's been a lot of responsibility with David at home. I've been thinking about that. As they get older they need something different. David is forty-four.

Robert: The most important thing for David is stability. My kids will do whatever they can for him. But for me, my soul is clean. I shed tears when I came out of the attorney's office. I'm on go-away time now; he's going to be here. Age catches up with you and we prepared for that.

Robert: I was a principal when the education law passed. I've never felt that all special ed children should be in contained settings. The least restrictive situation for children is to be treated like any normal child. They may be academically slow. You group them according to their abilities in reading, or you group them according to their math and social skills. Children are usually more normal than they are abnormal. I'm a firm believer that you must integrate these kids as much as possible. If they're in the community, why does the school have to separate them? As a principal, I had a tremendous role to play—as an advocate. Especially for low achieving, misbehaving kids. If you want to get rid of a kid, let them be slow, let them be a behavior problem, and you'll find every resource in the world—to get them out of a classroom. Well, I'm just the opposite. You have to change—that kid's not going to change. I had more of a problem teaching teachers how to work with urban kids, but I applied some of the same standards. Parents must have options. Do they want their kid in a special room, or would they prefer an ungraded room, or a more open environment? Other parents have it; we should have it too. When I enrolled those children after we got that special ed law, I said look at their age, look at their grade—I integrated as much as I could. Some teachers didn't even know they were special ed until the IEP's needed to be done. In the Individual Evaluations you set up the skills you want the child to have. It's not just for the teacher, it's for the parent and the child. It's a cooperative relationship.

some of these kids have – we'd be in a perfect world.

SCHOOLS' NEW COORDINATOR:

'Plain Talk' for Intergroup Ties

ROBERT BASS, NEW INTERGROUP-RELATIONS COORDINATOR, RELAXED WITH FAMILY
The children were, from left—Mary, 7; David, 4 (held by Mrs. Bass), and Robert, Jr., 6

By BOB MONAHAN

Robert A. Bass, 37, will emphasize frankness and plain talk in his new job as coordinator of intergroup relations for the Seattle Public School, he said yesterday.

The appointment to the new post was announced last night at a School Board meeting at Queen Anne High School.

Yesterday, as he relaxed at home, 1622 31st Av., with his wife and three children, he discussed the need for free flow of ideas on race and other social problems connected with education.

"I'm the mailman now," he said. "I do want the opportunity to meet not only with Negro groups, but with Caucasian groups, to get our view out into the open."

Bass, who has been a counselor at Franklin High School, will be responsible for coordinating public-school efforts to create better understanding among persons of different racial, religious, cultural and economic backgrounds.

Part of his job will be leading the transfer program to correct racial imbalance in schools.

Bass, a Negro, favors the transfer program and will make recommendations on how it should be carried out.

"I think this offers my people an opportunity to be free," he said. "They know that they don't have to go to a particular school because they live in a certain area."

Bass was born in Pittsburg, Kas. He came here in 1957 from Port Arthur, Tex., where he taught industrial arts five years.

He holds a master's degree from Kansas State Teachers' College and has done additional graduate work at the University of Washington.

An Army veteran, he served in the Pacific in the Second World War.

Bass said he will work with teachers and parents in a program of stimulating the desire to learn in underprivileged and minority-group children.

"The only real opportunity for a Negro to make advancement is through education," he said.

Bass was selected by the School Board from among 24 applicants. A panel of citizens helped the board determine qualifications for the job.

Nadean: When I took David to Central School I had two other kids, who weren't in school yet. The other parents said they didn't want any kids in the school who were "capable"—different than the disabled ones. So they weren't going to let me go to the school because of Mary and Bobby. I said, "What do you do with your kids at home?—you don't separate them." They didn't want the normal kids. I was the only one that brought my other kids. I knew David needed to go some place and not just be at home. So I asked them to give me some rooms, and they did. I put Bobby and Mary in a room, and then the teachers worked with David.

Rosco: Now I'm going to get into diversity. I don't know how many minorities were involved in ARC. If you study most of us, you will find out we are home people. We care for our own; it's always been that way. Our family went into education. We learned about services, we knew that we could go out to the university and get certain skills, we learned how you write up a certain kind of will—so you can protect your child. Now here's a good definition of education: Education is the ability that you have to use all the resources to your advantage. That's what it is. That's what a kid has to learn. In school, the child should learn how to use the teacher to their advantage. Not the teacher the other way. You need to use the system to your best advantage.

Robert: What you don't want to do is put your child in an institution. We, on a trial basis had him stay at Buckley. But, oh, to leave him there. When he came home it was the best day of my life. That's warehousen' these kids. I think we're closer as a family because of it. There has to be a lot of give and take. There is a learning relationship that we go through too with this child. It's a very intimate relationship. There is something you give up to have a child like this in your home. It changed me. I retired as soon as I could so I could spend more time with David and my family.

Nadean: You never know what's going to happen in life. When I first realized David had a medical problem I thought, why me? Why did this have to happen to me? I must have done something. Then I thought, I'm special because God gave me this child. He picked me to be this child's mother, and I've been going on from there.

Education Editor

A philosophical struggle about the form of public education is being fought throughout the nation and here in Seattle.

The issue is "alternative education."

This wasn't an exercise in lobbying
or political science. From our viewpoint
it was a matter of life and death.
It happened all the time. A kid left on
the doorstep of a state institution, or
abandoned at a downtown department store
with a bag of clothes. And then there is
the father that puts a gun to the
child's head and then his own. That's
the result of not having a mandatory
education law!

—Katie Dolan

Education for All

It is the paramount duty of the State to make ample provision for the education of all children residing within its borders, without distinction or preference on account of race, color, caste, or sex.

—Preamble to the State Constitution, Adopted 1889

Cecile Lindquist: We were coming out of what we called the "church basement" school era where we were given free space for classrooms. These were really grassroots operations. Parents started them and they were starting all over the country—everyone used the same terminology. In the Seattle area we had about four small programs. We were all applying for money. The state monies available at the time were the Epton dollars. It came from legislation sponsored by state Senator Kathryn Epton—who had a child with a disability. If parents could get a son or daughter on a wait list for an institution—even though they never intended to place their child there—they were eligible for the funds. This was a heartbreaking thing for parents to do, but it was a way these alternative programs could be supported.

Fred Fontana, who had a parent of a child with a disability in one of these programs, sat on the board of the Boeing Employees Good Neighbor Fund. He suggested to us that we pull the schools together and apply. They gave us $20,000 and this started Northwest Center. It was a zillion dollars to us. By consolidating we had more families involved and more people who had to be served. It gave us clout and it made us able to convince our United States senators, Warren Magnuson and Henry Jackson, to have some federal surplus World War II property given to Northwest Center. So for the first time we had space and funds. The Northwest Center Board convinced the Seattle Public schools: since you don't want these children the least you can do is send in some teachers for guidance.

When Katie, Evelyn, Janet, and I began to talk, I was president of the Board of the Center. They were very active in the Mother's Guild and we were constantly struggling to keep the Center glued together.

There were about 80 of us in the Mother's Guild of Northwest Center. We organized an annual bazaar and dozens of fundraising events to support our programs. Because so many of our children were school aged, we began talking about expanding the education budget. The Seattle Parks Department was the only community public or private program which never turned our kids away, and we began to think we should be developing legislation to provide more funding to Park Departments statewide for special programs. Janet had a connection with Wes Uhlman, a state legislator, who sponsored our idea for a bill. It didn't go anywhere but we gota taste for the legislative process. —Evelyn Chapman

Bill Requires Education for All

BY SUE LOCKETT

"2800 school-age children aren't receiving any education through the state. We realize it's more difficult to educate a handicapped child. But these are the children who need it most."

When Education for All organized to put a bill through the legislature, a state official warned his associates, "You may as well give in, I know these women and they won't quit."

For 11 months they haven't quit, and now they're in the midst of a telephone campaign to jar their bill out of the legislature's House Rules Committee.

The bill, HJR 90, is "to ensure that all handicapped children . . . shall have the opportunity for an appropriate education at public expense as guaranteed to them by the Constitution of this state."

E. F. A. executive committee member Cecile Lindquist recapped the steps taken by her group, especially her fellow-committee members (three mothers of handicapped children and two University of Washington law students).

She said, "The word homework is used a lot in Olympia. That's what much of our work was — boring, dogged, plugging away at getting information and support behind the proposed bill.

"We're into the more exciting part now — talking to individual legislators and watchdogging it through all the committees. But we've come to realize how important the non-glamorous preliminary steps are."

The first step was obtaining a legal opinion on the rights of handicapped children to public education. The assistant attorney general's opinion read: "We can conceive of no basis for construing the term 'all children' to exclude those with physical or mental handicaps."

Until then, the E. F. A. board had been considering a court case to test the constitutionality of the present "permissive" state law which says a school district may provide a education for the handicapped child.

The proposed bill would say must provide education for the handicapped through one of three options by 1973. 1) The district may provide the program itself. 2) It may contract with another district to provide a joint program. 3) It may contract with an existing agency specializing in programs for the retarded.

Through any of the options, the handicapped child would be guaranteed an education. And the parents would receive their fair return on their school taxes, Mrs. Lindquist said.

Legal opinion in hand, the E.F.A. approached the governor's office for a statewide survey to find how many school-aged handicapped are not participating in any program.

Working through the departments of public instruction and institutions, the governor's budget director came up with a total of 2,800 children between the ages of 6 and 18 who are not receiving any public schooling.

The budget office estimated the cost of starting programs for these children at approximately $5½ million over the next two years.

E.F.A. passed its next milestone when Governor Evans requested that amount in both his State of the State and his Budget messages to the legislature.

Law students George Breck and Bill Dussalult checked into the laws in other states and wrote the first draft of the bill.

Breck said, "On the whole, Washington compares pretty well. We're not downgrading the efforts already being made but now it's time to include everyone. About half the states have some kind of mandatory education law."

Another preliminary step was obtaining the support of the State Department of Public Instruction and of the chairman of the Joint Committee on Education—John Metcalf. Democratic Senator Martin Durkan also was an early supporter.

Thus the bill went before the House Rules Committee with endorsements from leaders in both political parties, the governor's office, the State Department of Public Instruction and numerous organizations of parents and professionals.

Mrs. Lindquist said, "That's where all the drudgery paid off. It sailed through the Rules Committee and sailed through Appropriations. We hit our only setback when it was returned to Rules and we were too complacent to contact each legislator.

"This time the Rules Committee, which had passed it right through before, voted to hold it up for further study. Now we're calling each committee member and explaining the importance of the bill.

"We're also urging all our friends and supporting organizations to telegram or call their legislators in behalf of the bill."

Mrs. Lindquist said, "We realize it's more difficult to educate a handicapped child. But these are the children who need it most. So do their parents."

Seattle Post-Intelligencer, February 21, 1971, page 4

Seattle Post-Intelligencer, May 11, 1971, page 10, editorial

SEATTLE P.I.

Handicapped Education

In the flurry of activity that accompanied the closing hours of the just concluded special session of the State Legislature, the Senate, by a 45-2 vote, approved a House-passed measure which will require all school districts to provide special education for all handicapped children of common school age.

Inasmuch as Governor Evans supported the "Education for All" measure from the outset of the regular legislative session, his signing of the bill into law will provide meaningful education to handicapped children, many of whom have never been in a real classroom situation.

We are pleased to see this significant measure approved and not shunted aside by the legislature as it rapidly moved toward closure this past weekend.

Too long have some handicapped youngsters missed out on educational opportunities. Tight budgets and limited facilities have precluded these children from having an "appropriate education" at public expense as guaranteed to them by the Constitution of this state. An appropriate education is one that is directed to the unique needs, abilities, and limitation of the handicapped children.

SO WITH THE passage of this legislation, an important gap in the state's total educational picture hopefully will be closed. On July 1, 1973, State Superintendent of Public Instruction will have the authority to implement this legislation which will allow all handicapped children the opportunity to develop to their full potentials.

© Seattle Times, Feb 8, 1971, page A12, editorial

SEATTLE TIMES

The state's 'paramount duty'

A BEDROCK provision in this state's Constitution proclaims that "it is the paramount duty of the state to make ample provision for the education of all children residing within its borders . . ."

This year, however, at least 2,800 school-age children in the state are not receiving education of any kind.

These are youngsters in various communities where there are no school programs for the retarded, emotionally disturbed or the physically handicapped.

The 1971 Legislature, however, is being asked to eliminate this gap. Bills have been introduced to require all local districts to provide programs for handicapped children either in the public schools or under contract with existing agencies, residential schools or approved homes.

Governor Evans' recommended budget includes $5 million for this purpose and the implementing legislation has impressive sponsorship from lawmakers in both parties.

The measures merit early approval by the full Legislature to correct an injustice and to meet the constitutional mandate that all children receive an appropriate educational opportunity.

A Toast To The Legislators With Love And Homemade Bread

BY DONNA JEAN CARROLL

Staff Home Economist

"We did it with love and homemade b r e a d," said Mrs. Duane (Katie) Dolan, during the fourth annual Legislator's Luncheon held recently in the Nile Temple at Seattle Center.

Katie, publicity chairman for the Northwest Center Mothers' Guild, attributes passage of H.B. 90, mandatory education act for handicapped children, to these luncheons.

A Legislator's Luncheon is a high-noon affair at which parents and friends of the mentally retarded entertain their legislators and inform them of the needs of retarded citizens and their families.

With Champagne in hand, Katie proposed a toast, "We'd like to toast all of you who helped us pass H.B. 90 when money was tight and education was in difficulty. God bless you."

The NCMG, sponsor of the luncheon, is one of the first organizations to use t h i s method for lobbying bills through the Legislature.

As in past years, the luncheon lasted exactly one hour, featuring the home cooking of its members — s e r v e d potluck-style. See some of the recipes below.

With a hall, some good cooks and hard workers, an eye to publicity and several public speakers, you, too, can hold a luncheon.

The chief rule is to do every bit of the work yourselves and get everything donated or for cost.

If any group would like a complete outline of how to go about it, write to Northwest Center for the Retarded, Pier 91, Bldg. 270, Seattle 98119.

The outline, an 11-page pamphlet, "How To Give A Legislator's Luncheon," with tips on the what, why, who, where, when and how,

LEGISLATORS CELEBRATE H.B. 90 VICTORY

David Wood, left, and Joseph Epler, third left, spoon up

SALAD IN A BASKET OF HOT ITALIAN BREAD

costs $1. Profits from sales go toward programs at the Center.

Salad In A Basket

⅓ cup margarine or salad dressing
2 tablespoons milk
2 tablespoons chopped chives
½ teaspoon dry mustard
¼ teaspoon salt
Dash pepper
1 loaf (9 inches in diameter) Italian bread
1 jar (5 ounces) cheese spread with garlic
½ stick (¼ cup) butter, softened
6 hard-cooked eggs
1 cup cherry tomatoes, halved
1 small green pepper, chopped

Blend first 6 ingredients in small bowl and chill for 30 minutes. With sharp knife, cut a circle around bread about 1 inch from edge. Lift off top and scoop out bread, leaving a 1-inch shell.

In small bowl, cream the cheese spread and butter until smooth. Spread evenly over inside of bread loaf.

Wrap loaf in foil and bake at 400 degrees 10 minutes or until cheese is golden and bubbly. Combine eggs, tomatoes and green pepper. Fold in dressing. Spoon mixture into bread "basket." Cut into thick wedges to serve.

Note: An electric knife is desirable for cutting.

Potato Spice Cake

2 cups sifted all-purpose flour
5 teaspoons unsweetened cocoa
2 teaspoons baking powder
1 teaspoon cinnamon
½ teaspoon salt
½ teaspoon cloves
1 cup butter, softened
2 cups sugar
1 cup mashed potatoes
4 eggs, separated
1 cup coarsely chopped pecans
1 cup raisins
¾ cup maraschino cherries, drained, chopped

Preheat oven to 350 degrees. Grease and flour two 9-inch layer cake pans or one 9x13-inch pan. Sift flour with cocoa, baking powder, cinnamon, salt and cloves.

In large bowl, with electric mixer at medium speed, cream butter with sugar, potatoes and yolks until light and fluffy.

At low speed, gradually beat in flour mixture 1 minute. Beat egg whites until stiff peaks form, then gently fold into batter. Stir in nuts, raisins and cherries.

Bake 40 minutes or until tester, when inserted, comes out clean. Cool. Frost with a caramel icing.

Old-Fashioned Pot Roast

6-to-10-pound pot roast
1 package dry onion soup mix

Wipe pot roast with a damp cloth. Place in Dutch oven. Don't add water. Sprinkle with onion soup mix. Cover. Bake at 250 or 275 degrees for 8 to 10 hours.

Buttery Dill Rolls

1 package dry yeast
3 teaspoons dried dill weed
5 cups buttermilk-biscuit mix
Soft butter

Dissolve yeast in 1⅓ cups warm water with dill weed. Add biscuit mix, mixing well. Turn out onto floured surface, kneading until smooth.

Roll out dough to ¼-inch thickness. Spread generously with butter. Cut 2-inch rounds; place buttered side up on baking sheet. Top with remaining rounds, buttered side down. Let rise in warm place about 20 minutes. Bake at 425 degrees for 8 minutes or until golden brown.

Saucy Meat Balls

3 or 4 pounds ground beef
1 package ground beef mix
1 package onion soup mix
1½ cups bread crumbs
2 eggs, beaten
1 can (8 ounces) tomato sauce
Meat Sauce

To the ground beef, add beef mix, onion soup mix, bread crumbs, eggs and tomato sauce. Mix thoroughly. Shape into balls. Brown in hot oil in skillet; drain off excess fat. Add Tomato-Onion Meat Sauce and simmer 25 minutes, stirring occasionally. Makes 6 to 7 dozen meat balls, using about a teaspoonful for each.

Tomato-Onion Meat Sauce: Mix together 1 package onion soup mix, 1 package mushroom soup mix, 2 cans (8 ounces each) tomato sauce and 1½ cups water. Heat thoroughly.

Tori Picks
Ginger Marinade

½ cup soy sauce
¼ cup sake or Sherry wine
½ teaspoon ginger
¼ cup sugar

Cut breast of chicken in 1-inch pieces. Sprinkle with Ginger Marinade and let set overnight in refrigerator.

Impale one or two pieces of chicken on each wooden pick, coat in flour and brown in hot, greased skillet. Then dip each piece in mixture of soy sauce, sake, ginger and sugar. Place picks in roasting pan. Bake at 350 degrees 30 minutes, turning occasionally.

Ginger Marinade: Sprinkle chicken pieces with ginger, sugar and soy sauce.

Cherry tomatoes and green pepper add color

67

—P-I Photos by Bob Miller

VARIED HOME COOKING FEATURED
Food lobbies bills through legislature

The ARC asked us to join them in a Legislator's Luncheon. They had tried to hold them before but no one ever came. I asked my friend Fred Dore, who was the Chair of the powerful Senate Ways and Means Committee, as well as part of the Justice Committee to come, but he was the only legislator who came. Afterwards he said to me, "Katie, if you want to do this right—you gals are swell cooks and you're a super organizer—you've put hundreds of parties and plays together. Here's what you do. It should last one hour, you have every parent call their legislator and you tell them you're going to have home-cooked food. If you have to go and pick those legislators up. That's what you do. You introduce each one, you'll have the newspapers and televisions there. You give them a ten minute talk with a handout about what you want them to do, they eat, and that's it." We followed his directions. We set the tables up like a political convention—each representing a legislative district so the legislators and their constituents could sit together. All the TV stations and newspapers covered the event. Those lunches were so popular, we had judges and people from Social Security begging for invitations— I mean everybody wanted to be there. And we got our point across! —Katie Dolan

The Education for All Law, House Bill 90, came out of years of frustration of trying to run good programs and it came to a head at Northwest Center. It also meant that parents could no longer depend upon "professionals" but must do things for themselves. They took over the Board at the Center and created programs; it just grew out of this environment of action sparked by years of rejection.

We didn't know what we wanted at first. Katie found two students through the University of Washington Law School— George Breck and Bill Dussault. We became a committee of six—though we sought out people to guide us. We talked with education leaders, labor leaders, state legislators, and the governor and his staff. However, we also had frustrating experiences trying to convince some people that these children had a right to an education. Our idea was that we must have a broader view of education, not only what we usually envision as hard academics. Education is the whole child, and whatever we can do to enhance that child's potential—whatever that might be—is education. I put in a request to Governor Dan Evans. We needed a survey of all the children with disablilities in the state who were not getting a public education. We needed the research to back us up. The Governor assigned it to the Superintendent of Public Instruction, who came back with a figure of 5,367 children, which turned out to be very low. There were many families who weren't being served, and were on their own. They were out of our network. But this was a beginning. The survey became the basis for $5 million being allocated in the Governor's budget for unserved children with disabilities.

HOUSE BILL NO. 90

State of Washington   by Representatives Brouillet, Hoggins, Chatalas, Kirk,
42nd Regular Session   Merrill, Lynch, Grant, Conner, Thompson, Marsh,
                                       Backstrom, Bagnariol, Bauer, Beck, Ceccarelli,
                                       Charnley, Douthwaite, Farr, Gallagher, King, Luders,
                                       Martinis, Marzano, Mentor, McCormick, O'Brien, Paris,
                                       Rosellini, Williams, Wojahn and Litchman
                                       (by Joint Committee on Education request, Executive
                                       request and Superintendent of Public Instruction request)
Read first time January 13, 1971, and referred to Committee on Education and Libraries.

1   AN ACT Relating to educational opportunities for all handicapped
2   children; amending section 28A.13.010, chapter 223, Laws of
3   1969 ex. sess. as amended by section 2, chapter 2, Laws of
4   1969 ex. sess. and RCW 28A.13.010; amending section
5   28A.13.020, chapter 223, Laws of 1969 ex. sess. and RCW
6   28A.13.020; amending section 28A.13.030, chapter 223, Laws of
7   1969 ex. sess. and RCW 28A.13.030; amending section
8   28A.13.040, chapter 223, Laws of 1969 ex. sess. and RCW
9   28A.13.040; amending section 28A.13.050, chapter 223, Laws of
10   1969 ex. sess. and RCW 28A.13.050; amending section
11   28A.24.100, chapter 223, Laws of 1969 ex. sess. and RCW
12   28A.24.100; adding new sections to chapter 28A.13 RCW; adding
13   a new section to chapter 28A.41 RCW; providing penalties; and
14   making an effective date.

15 BE IT ENACTED BY THE LEGISLATURE OF THE STATE OF WASHINGTON:

16   NEW SECTION. Section 1. It is the purpose of this 1971
17 amendatory act to ensure that all handicapped children as defined in
18 section 2 of this 1971 amendatory act shall have the opportunity for
19 an appropriate education at public expense as guaranteed to them by
20 the Constitution of this state.

21   Sec. 2. Section 28A.13.010, chapter 223, Laws of 1969 ex.
22 sess. as amended by section 2, chapter 2, Laws of 1969 ex. sess. and
23 RCW 28A.13.010 are each amended to read as follows:

24   There is established in the office of the superintendent of
25 public instruction a division of special ((educational aid))
26 education for handicapped children, to be known as the division for
27 handicapped children.

-1-

HB 90

1   Handicapped children are those children in school or out of
2   school who are temporarily or permanently retarded in normal
3   educational processes by reason of physical or mental handicap, or by
4   reason of ((social or)) emotional maladjustment, or by reason of
5   other handicap, and those children who have specific learning and
6   language disabilities resulting from perceptual-motor handicaps,
7   including problems in visual and auditory perception and integration.
8   ((: PROVIDED, That))

9   The superintendent of public instruction shall require each
10 school district in the state to insure an appropriate educational
11 opportunity for all handicapped children of common school age. The
12 superintendent of public instruction, by rule and regulation, shall
13 establish for the purpose of excess cost funding, as provided in this
14 1971 amendatory act, functional definitions of the various types of
15 handicapping conditions and eligibility criteria for handicapped
16 programs. For the purposes of this chapter, an appropriate education
17 is defined as an education directed to the unique needs, abilities,
18 and limitations of the handicapped children.

19 This section shall not be construed as in any way limiting the
20 powers of local school districts set forth in section 7 of this 1971
21 amendatory act.

22 No child shall be removed from the jurisdiction of juvenile
23 court for training or education under this chapter without the
24 approval of the superior court of the county.

25 Sec. 3. Section 28A.13.020, chapter 223, Laws of 1969 ex.
26 sess. and RCW 28A.13.020 are each amended to read as follows:

27 The superintendent of public instruction shall appoint an
28 administrative officer of ((such)) the division. The administrative
29 officer, under the direction of the superintendent of public
30 instruction, shall coordinate and supervise the program of special
31 ((aid)) education for all handicapped children in the school
32 districts of the state. He shall cooperate with ((county and))
33 intermediate school district superintendents and local school

-2-

"Don't worry, what can four mothers in tennis shoes do?"

George and Bill researched laws around the country. We realized that our own state constitution was very strong about education. Katie had a family friend who was a state senator, and she asked him to get us an attorney general's opinion—a citizen can't get one, but an elected official can. We think the attorney general was leary of what it would mean, but yes, these children did have a right to an education under constitutional law. Our constitution is very clear—these children have a right to a public education. We have one of the strongest constitutions in the country. Article 9 says it is the paramount duty of the state to make ample provision for the education of all children. Isn't that wonderful—it's beautiful. Our children had been denied what was rightfully theirs!

At first we thought about suing for failure to follow the state constitution. We learned that parents in Pennsylvania were considering a law suit to provide education for children with severe mental retardation. This became PARC (Pennsylvania Association for Retarded Children) v. the State of Pennsylvania. We discussed it at length. Should we sue? We concluded that we would have a better opportunity to bring about change

Janet and I researched every single state legislator in the house and senate. We knew who had a child who had died perhaps—or who had a child, or a niece or nephew or brother with a disability. We knew who had been a minister, or a social worker, or which one's wives had been special education teachers. We knew their past voting record. We did this research so we could talk to each and every legislator at their level of understanding. It was crazy but we knew everything about everybody and we each assigned ourselves to different ones. —Katie Dolan

in our state through the legislative process. We began the process of writing the legislation. It went through many drafts. We met every week for two years. We named our comittee Education for All. Education is a states rights issue. The federal government can intervene if a state violates the equal protection amendment—which gives everyone equal protection under the law. You cannot be denied the right to something that someone else has. So in essence it was a civil rights issue.

Behind everything we did was the Northwest Center mother's guild. They were on the phone, or organizing a bake sale. They called their legislators. The parents were looked at as rabble-rousers. We set up the bill so it not only mandated education, but also transportation, and we wrote in penalties for failure to comply. When House Bill 90 was being debated in the Rules Committee, an amendment was introduced—to take out the penalties. We engineered a House floor debate and we gave every member of the House of Representatives one sheet of paper. It said don't vote for this—it will hurt the children—with a list of reasons. The amendment was defeated and the bill passed! —Janet Taggart

The head of the State Labor Council, Joe Davis, really helped us—he was sympathetic because one of his key staff, a lobbyist, Larry Kenney, had a daughter with a developmental disability. Joe told us we should introduce our bill as a request of the Senate or House Education Committee, or by the Governor, or by the State Superintendent of Public Instruction. We took his advice and did all four! Representative Frank Brouillet, chair of the House Education Committee, was the prime sponsor of the house bill. Senator Jack Metcalf, Chair of the Senate Education Comittee, was prime sponsor of the senate bill.

The Education for All Committee traveled statewide to secure key sponsors and gain support from parents, disability organizations, legislators, and the media. We also worked continuously to neutralize opposition. Some parents of children without disabilities thought the money given to unserved children would reduce service to their children. And some parents of children with disabilities were just afraid—especially of change. A critical part of our strategy was to have a constant presence at the State Capital. One or more of us was at the legislature every day during the sessions. We gathered and gave information and brought it back to our weekly meetings. One day we talked to 96 members of the House of Representatives to vote against an amendment to remove the sanctions from the Bill. Then we mobilized again to defeat an amendment that proposed to remove school bus service.

After the Bill passed in 1971 we were invited to San Francisco and to Washington, D.C., to participate in drafting the federal law. What we were doing, this struggle for education rights, was happening all over the country. The authors of the federal legislation took the name—Education for All—from our bill. We sold it on civil rights and the Constitution. Everything we do for the children will help the society in the long run. More schooling means more independence.

Things came together in the '60s and early '70s that made it possible for this bill to pass. We had a President—John Kennedy, who had a sister with a disability—the Civil Rights movement, and especially Brown vs. Board of Education. It was a time when parents began to question conventional wisdom and authority—the authority of their doctors, the authority of their schools and churches, the authority of the system. Our job as citizens is to come together to figure out what we want and work together to get it. It was exhausting work but it was also exciting and satisfying. In 1975 the national law—Public Law 94-142, passed ensuring the right to education for all children with disablilities in our Nation.

Signing House Bill 90, 1971. Janet Taggart, Katie Dolan, Cecile Lindquist, Governor Daniel Evans, Evelyn Chapman, George Breck, and William Dussault 1990 (inset)

We had real talent as a team; three of us were mothers with firsthand knowledge of disability. Evelyn was brilliant, she had experience as a legal secretary and as a budget analyst and could read any law. She was also fearless and would go behind the scenes and talk to anybody. Janet had, well, a socialist background and knew how to connect with people. She was also a fine journalist. She wrote stories about our progress and fed them to the press. They were delighted, they didn't have to do any work, and our story got published verbatim. We had Cecile, who was the Governor's cousin, she had worked with the "establishment." She knew lobbyists. She was a teacher and an administrator and she was working with the Experimental Education Unit at the University of Washington. We pushed her out front because she had been active politically. I was the dramatist. I was an actress. I'd had a TV show. I knew how to handle the PR. I knew how to organize events and I had lots of connections, both in society and with legislators.—Katie Dolan

PARENTS LEAD CRUSADE
FOR THE RETARDED

From the beginning, We talked about this as a civil rights movement for the disabled.

Bill Dussault: We wanted to obtain recognition of a constitutional right to education for all children under the Washington State Constitution. The educational and civil rights ideas were intertwined.

It was not an education bill that became a civil rights bill, or the other way around. We understood this was the first step in creating a premise of respect for people who were different. Historically there had never been anyone outside the educational environment having the right to define the content of education. Curriculum was exclusively the province of the educators. What we described was equal sharing of control between the parents of the children with disabilities and the educators. There must be agreement over the content of education. The process of development of the IEP (Individualized Educational Program) required equal participation between the parents of the student and the District. If either side disagreed, either side can go to hearing. Historically control over educational programming had always been 90/10 in favor of the educators. The concept that parents could have an equal right to participate in decisions about their child's learning was revolutionary. This is not something that the education establishment did. This was something that was done to education.

In retrospect it was extraordinary that the work for House Bill 90 wasn't done by paid lobbyists, even in those days. It was also very unusual to not have the bill come from the educational environment. While we came up with the legal concepts, I would call my colleague George Breck and I super scriveners. We were part of a team, we wrestled with concepts, but everything we did always went back through Janet, Katie, Evelyn, and Cecile. They were tough, and "beat us up" more than once over the specific ideas. My initial task was as the researcher. I ran the education codes for fifty states. In most states, the law said that children with disabilities were allowed to go to public school if the local school district and/or the state said it was OK. They were called "permissive programs." So if the local folks were willing, they could choose to serve none, some, or all of the children they considered "handicapped." "We'll take the blind kids, but we won't take those 'other' kids." State education codes indicated that children who were "afflicted with loathsome and contagious diseases" including epilepsy and cerebral palsy were not allowed to be served. This is a legislative quote. Many of those laws had been written in the '20s under the influence of the Eugenics movement and had never been updated. The ignorance reflected in the legislation was breathtaking. The ones we were most interested in serving were the ones that had always been always excluded, the children with more profound disabilities. The response from the educational establishment was, "Oh, you want to put 'those' kids in school?" We said, "Yes, all of them, zero reject." There were no states at that point with a Zero Reject law. We were the first. It meant that everyone had a right to an education.

They always said our children are uneducable, therefore they don't qualify for the education rights. As parents, we weren't sure really, until we found Margot Thornley, a teacher at Fircrest, who brought us a film she had made teaching children with profound handicaps. The name of her movie was Every Child Can Learn. *She was using her own version of behavioral techniques. In the film, it was so obvious because you see them learning. I interviewed her for an education program on TV and we showed the film. We brought her to a hearing in Olympia—we played this film over and over at many hearings. —Katie Dolan*

One of the arguments was, "You can't mean those kids who are comatose." We determined that there were about twelve such children in the state at that time and so we said— "OK, those too!"

The Barefoot Schoolboy laws, written in the 1890s, were the first compulsory attendance laws, and they existed in all 50 states. But children with disabilities were excused from mandatory attendance. The formal structure of Special Education in America came into being in the early 1900s with the distinction between children who were educable and trainable. Those who were considered educable were sometimes allowed in educational programs. Those who were considered trainable were seldom allowed.

In Pennsylvania, the distinction between educable and trainable children was finally debunked in the 1972 PARC Federal District Court litigation. The expert witnesses who testified in the case on behalf of the children said that there was no distinction in terms of education technologies; everyone was educable. The distinction between the two so-called categories of children had much more to do with the skills of the educators. Most states referred to these children as defective; it was a common term in the state legislature until the 1970s. Other common terms used included "idiots, imbeciles, and feebleminded" which relate to later categories of mild, moderate and severe mental retardation.

In the 1890s the Fernald School for Feebleminded Children was founded in Massachusetts. It came from a movement started by Samuel Gridley Howe in the 1840s. It was the beginning of the state school or institutions movement, which included schools for "improvable" children, or children with mild disabilities. Some early educators believed that these children could be educated—through special educational techniques. Though there were successful examples, the concept somehow became perverted, or perhaps the educators lost sight of their goals. Ultimately these early schools became custodial institutions, in effect segregating and isolating large numbers of individuals with disabilities. The irony is that the Fernald State School, like so many others, with all their wonderful intentions became more like warehouses, much like an English poorhouse.

The Eugenics movement, founded in America in the '20s, also fueled these ideas—I might also add it influenced Hitler's writing in *Mien Kampf*. It encouraged registration and sterilization programs for the disabled. It is most starkly reminisced in Justice Oliver Wendell Holmes's well-known and embarrassing opinion, written for the Supreme Court in a case

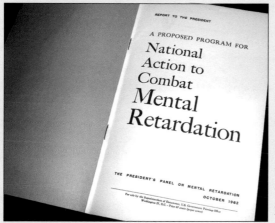

called Buck v. Bell. He wrote, "three generations of idiots is enough" when he allowed the forced sterilization of a mother who was "mentally retarded." He argued that "mental retardation" was hereditary and needed to be controlled. It was, until recently, a common policy to sterilize women in the state institutions. We had one client who described it as, "Tying her bellybutton to her backbone." This is the stuff you find along the way when you start to look at this as a civil rights issue. Realizations hit you and you think, "By God! How could they do that to any generic population?" You can't look at it as just a few women, because they are doing it by categorical definition. Once an individual is given the label, dehumanizing consequences will follow.

The importance of the Washington State law goes way beyond what occurred in this state. You have to view it in the context of the creation of the entire civil rights movement for individuals with disabilities. The Washington law coupled with the PARC case in Pennsylvania created the same momentum for the disabled that Brown v. Board of Education created for Black kids. 1973 was a seminal year. That year in the Federal session you saw:

1. *The introduction of The Education for All Handicapped Children Act, P.L. 94-142*

2. *Title V of the Rehabilitation Act (P.L. 93-112), which included section 504, the first of the anti-discrimination acts.*

3. *The Federal Highway Aid Act of 1973 (P.L. 93-87 and The Urban Mass Transit Act (P.L. 93-503), requiring increased accessibility in public transportation*

This new momentum to recognize the rights of individuals with disabilities came out of Congress, largely through the efforts of Senator Harrison Williams of N.J., Jennings Randolph, West Va., Jacob Javitz, N.Y., and Ted Kennedy, Mass. So '73 was an explosive year for the establishment of rights. But it was built on decades of work. In 1962 a report was issued by the Kennedy Administration outlining a series of programs for the developmentally disabled—we are still implementing recommendations from that report 50 years later. In fact it predicted what happened in 1973, and the steps that led up to it in the preceding five years here in Washington State, in Pennsylvania, and in DC. On the East Coast, the progress was made by litigation. On the West Coast, it was made by legislation. There was a confluence. Children with disabilities did not exist as a discrete population in a federal sense, with the same rights as other children, until 1973. We started the creation of that recognition with this bill. It became a public law in 1975

They were doing things we
never imagined possible . . .
but you see they were away
from home.

—Myrtle McNary

About Citizens

When Jeffrey McNary moved into his first group home, he communicated through gestures that he was unsatisfied with his appearance. The support staff soon learned he wanted to grow a mustache. Jeffery had lived at home with his family who had never realized he wanted this change. His sister Sherry said, "There were so many things we didn't know about Jeff—in many ways, we learned who he was when he left home. It's possible to love someone too much, so you don't see who they are and what they need."

Two significant pieces of legislation—The Education for All Handicapped Children Act in 1975 and the Americans with Disabilities Act in 1990—initiated great change for people with disabilities, and also enabled "mainstream" Americans to become more aware of the rights citizens with disabilities have historically been denied. Though People First, the first self-advocacy group organized by and for people with cognitive disabilities was founded in 1974, the principles of self advocacy are only slowly (though steadfastly) being inserted into the mainstream of American life—through legislation, political action, and personal example.

"About Citizens" continues the chronicle of family and disability but emphasizes the ways individuals with cognitive disabilities are creating lives in the community and imagining their own futures. It also describes some of the ways families situated their family member—recreational activities, jobs, and housing. While the stories present remarkable achievements, they are also reminders of the challenges that remain. It also suggests the ways individuals must work together to invent a form of citizenship that respects and supports the humanity of all.

Summer 57

Terry 4 1/2 yrs. Marie 15 mos.

Marie Strausbaugh

Vivian: When Marie was young, this lady started a Camp Fire group for kids who were handicapped. Marie was thrilled! They went twice, but the woman gave it up because she got pregnant. The kids were so disappointed. So Herb said to Marie, "Maybe I can teach you kids square dancing." So it started with our little Camp Fire group. The Parks Department let us use the room for free and then we had to get the boys. Herb had them once a week. He was a very patient man. I went along and made sure they stayed in their squares and helped organize them. They started out with one square and then they progressed. They loved it. They absolutely loved it. When he'd put on a record, they'd get really excited. We were used to raising money through bazaars and sales. Herb had a friend in the nursery business, so he bummed a bunch of plants and they sold them to make money. Once we had a talent show at one of the theaters. The first costumes the kids had came from money the Irish Rovers gave us. Later, we got these matching outfits donated from the Dummy Club—out of the clear-blue sky. We bought them the petticoats and the underpanties and the mothers made the dresses.

He knew they could do it. One was square to four hands, where you go one, two, three, four, and a lot more steps, and he couldn't get them to do it. And we prayed about it and the next morning he said, "God did it because he told them they were toy soldiers and that made a difference." There are other steps like right and left grand. Yes, and when you promenade you have to take hands or when you allamand right and left you go one way or the other in the circle.

We had a dancing group and we called them The Gypsy Squares. We went from campground to campground during different times of the year. There were various square-dance clubs and we'd bring our trailers and camp and then we'd dance in the hall. There would be games in the afternoon. It was a way of life and Marie just loved it.

Herb had a musical background. As a kid he was in the Paper Boys' Band. They paid 25 cents a week to use instruments. He started with the violin and then he went into the trumpet. When we started square dancing in '69, he'd always be where the caller was, asking about different things. There were about eight men who went to the caller's house to learn. They were all so scared, no one would try. My husband was the only one, and so he called.

In 1991 Herb found out he had cancer. He kept up with the square dancing until about '95. It was almost twenty two years. We took our kids to the state dance competition and we were the only retarded group invited to dance in the National Square Dancing Convention. People were there from all over the world! Herb always had these goals. He died in '99. I'm so proud of what he did. We all wished that someone would have taken over after he died.

Vivian Strausbaugh talks about Marie and Herb

He challenged them. I said, "You're pushing them too hard"

and he says, "They can learn. They can learn."

We never thought of putting Marie in an institution.
But, after we found out she had Down Syndrome
I thought, I'll never smile again.
I wouldn't let them take pictures at the hospital.
Our parish priest came to see me and told Herb to visit the
Bishop. Afterward Herb came back smiling and said,
"The Bishop said we have a little angel, a little saint."
In Ireland when someone is born like that, they say,
"Aren't you lucky that you have a little saint, a little angel."
I never went to see the Bishop.
I just knew I was never going to have her picture taken.
And now look at all the pictures. My goodness!

Northgate Journal

MAR 30 1980
TIMES

The Second Annual Square Dance-a-Thon to benefit the Muscular Dystrophy Association will be held from 1-10:30 p.m. Sunday in the I.B.E.W. Hall, 2700 First Ave. There will be live music by The Cross Cats, calling by a panel of callers and dancing by top groups in the Pacific Northwest. Whether you want to kibbitz or actually do some clogging, call 271-4760.

Vol. 26 No. 93
16 Pages
Wednesday, July 11, 1979

Herb's angels square off—'reely'

By BILL GELONECK

Off the dance floor Herb Strausbaugh is one of those nice, easy-going guys who you'd swear never raises his voice at anybody.

But on the dance floor, that all changes. Strausbaugh is in his element, there, calling the shots—dance routines, rather—as a professional square dance caller.

And heaven help you if you get out of step. Unless, of course, you're one of his "Swinging Angels." He might make a few exceptions in that case—but that doesn't mean he'll cut any corners.

All of Strausbaugh's "Swinging Angels," a gathering of several mentally handicapped children, are angels to him. It takes a lot of hard work, sure, and a lot of patience, but the smile that stretches across his face tells all.

But in his own words, "They're really something, and they're so appreciative. I get a lot of thank yous out of them that I probably wouldn't from others."

Strausbaugh and his wife, Vivian, Broadview residents, began teaching handicapped children square dancing in 1972. As he puts it, "I kinda fell into it, really," when a local mother-to-be called on him to help her organize a Camp Fire group for handicapped children. When she had to give up her idea for the birth of her child, Strausbaugh turned the program over strictly to...

as a kid? Y'know, we marched around stiff-like and all." He applied the gimmick to a "by-the-numbers" method of instruction: the children picked it up and loved it.

But the "Swinging Angels" do more than simply meet once a week at Thomson Junior High School for lessons. In late June they were invited to perform during the State Square Dancing Festival in Edmonds. They were the only group among several to receive a standing ovation, although they did not compete in the festival.

"A lot of other callers came up to congratulate Herb for the job he's done with the kids," says his wife, "and their everyday teachers are constantly asking what his secret is. They're always telling him how much they wish they could get the kids to pay attention in school the way they pay attention to Herb."

Strausbaugh, however, refuses to allow his wife to take a back seat; she works hard with the children, too, he says, right by his side.

"Don't let her kid you," he emphasizes. "She does an awful lot. She just doesn't like to admit it, that's all."

"I get too emotionally involved," she says sheepishly. "I worry about the kids a lot and sometimes I can't sleep."

Their daughter, Marie, also handicapped, is a member of...

THE "SWINGING ANGELS" keep in step with the tempo as their instructor and caller, Herb Strausbaugh (far right), puts them through the paces.

is put that record on and they all start beaming."

But there's more to the group than merely recognition, such as a graduation certificate each member receives for their September-through-June dance classes.

"It's social," says Vivian. "They like their peer group just like everyone else...

"They're all real hams," he says with a grin.

The Strausbaughs don't limit their square dancing lessons to the Angels. Several times a year they take their talents to nursing homes and convalescent centers. Wheelchairs are no barriers, either.

The doctors gave us so little information of what to expect. I nursed her for nine months until I couldn't any longer. Someone told us they smile at the age of six months. Her sister is three years older and I'm sure Marie learned much earlier from her. We didn't really think about her potential, we accepted her and lived with her day by day. We took her to Temple De Hirsch and Central School when she was five. We had a station wagon so I drove seven kids. I stayed at school and helped out in the classrooms. One psychologist once said it isn't important that your daughter can read CAT. But it is important that when you take her out, that she's not crawling on people's furniture. When she started at school I was thrilled. But the first day she came home with every kid's bad habit. She curled her fingers. She rocked back and forth. But when I asked her not to she stopped. At one of the schools they taught her how to make her bed. She won't come out of her room until her bed is made. I prayed that she would go to communion and she is very religious. She loves going to church; in fact one of our parish priests said she was the most religious retarded child he had ever seen. She still is.

Marie was born in 1956. I've often said I'd like to write a book. I had no preparation. I was in the hospital bed, enjoying the fact that I had no tummy and I hear footsteps—the clicking of a woman's heels and it stopped in my room. I opened my eyes and looked at this woman who had no smile and she said, "Do you notice anything different about your baby?" This was my second child and we'd noticed the shape of her eyes. "Do you notice anything else?" She kept persisting. By then my mind was, "What is she saying?" "Your daughter is mentally retarded. She's a Mongoloid." I didn't know what it meant, but after she said "retarded" I wasn't listening anymore. When I told Herb we had a retarded daughter, I remember I was laying on the bed and he put his head on my breast and he cried and he cried his heart out. He cried and cried and of course, I had been too. They told my husband to put her in an institution, except one doctor who said "Take her home and treat her like your other children." So that's what we did.

Lance Peake

Doreen: Lance was born in 1955. The pediatrician said he'd never progress, never learn anything, and I should put him in an institution. I mean he looked normal to me. Our family doctor was furious and said, "Take him home, I can't tell you how far he'll progress, every child is different." Lance was so active. Most Down's just lie there. Lance was all over the place. He climbed out of his crib before he could walk. The doctors really didn't know what to expect. I couldn't have put him in an institution—I don't care how bad he was. Lance did learn things—to walk, and feed himself, maybe a few months later than my other son. He learned to dress himself— to do his buttons and zippers. His speech was coming along. He would surprise us with the things he would come out with. We were encouraged that this child could learn.

My husband accepted Lance, but he died when Lance was two so he didn't really have to face the things we had to do. He had this cold and got so weak he could hardly walk. I somehow found a doctor one Saturday morning, but my husband passed away before he arrived. It was walking pneumonia. So I had to be home all the time. We got social security but it wasn't enough so I got a job at a temp agency.

He comes home every weekend. He's very neat ....

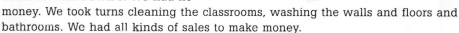

As my other son got older he wouldn't let me hire a babysitter. He would take care of his brother. I didn't know anything about retarded children, about where they went or what they did. When he was close to five, I had to do something.

I called the ARC and they told me to call this mother who wanted to start a preschool. It was the start of Central School. There were other children with Down's. We had no money. We took turns cleaning the classrooms, washing the walls and floors and bathrooms. We had all kinds of sales to make money.

They tried to teach the children things, but at that time they had the idea that these children couldn't learn so we should teach them hygiene and social skills. One teacher, Mary Hiramatsu, who also had a retarded boy in the school, taught them how to write their names and other things.

We had so many people wanting to come we contacted the public schools to ask for financial help. Instead, they selected ten children to go to Pacific School. This was a school for "slow learners." They picked the ones who could dress and go to the toilet by themselves. Lance was one of them. The classrooms were in a portable unit adjacent to the school. The "slow learners" were primarily economically disadvantaged kids, many of them Black. They were in the main building. Our kids would go over there for some things, but they were mostly segregated. The teachers were surprised. They thought they would have a bunch of idiots doing nothing. These kids were able to do a lot of things. They didn't teach them much in the way of reading and writing. Lance started there when he was ten. They could stay until they were twenty-one. But he got bored. So when he was eighteen I brought him to Northwest Center. They put him in a training program. He's been there ever since. He started in the laundry and he had no problem learning to run all the different machines. It was interesting to go there. They'd run this machine and the sheet would go around and come out the other side absolutely dry. Then the pillow cases would be run through. Then they decided they were loosing money on the laundry. What hit the Center financially was having to pay insurance for the people working. We said they don't need insurance; they all had Medicare and Medicaid. But they had to do it, so the program stopped.

He puts things away sometimes before I'm through using them.

He could have been way above what he is now. He doesn't read. They didn't believe in it. I'm sure he could; he understands symbols. Now, they teach them from the time they are really little. He's quite intelligent in a lot of ways. With electronics, you show him how to do something once on a TV or a stereo, he knows. I don't know how it works but he does!

Lance is forty-eight and he's lived at a group home for four years. The first night, I got a call, Lance is gone. I got in the car—the group home was about fifty blocks across two very busy streets. I thought maybe he'll remember. He's good at remembering things. So I drove the way we had gone before. No sign of him. We called the police; Lance always had his address with him. Well, Mr. Peake was cutting down to a different street and walking over to 105th. How he knew that, I don't know. On the third way around, here he is walking down Holman Road, his bowling bag in one hand and his overnight bag over his shoulder. I mean this is a kid that doesn't like to go for a walk! He was going at quite a pace. So I brought him home. Every night I got a phone call. He was sobbing, he wanted to come home. I kept trying to explain, Your mom's getting old, Lance, and I want you someplace where you'll be looked after nicely. But every night I got a phone call. I dreaded the phone ringing. Once he even faked chest pains. They called me and said they had taken him to the hospital. So here's Lance with all these things hooked up. The doctor is asking him, "Does this hurt?" And Lance is saying "no, no, no, no," nothing hurt. I told the doctor he is just pulling one on you. So we took him back to the group home and we told him no matter what you do you're going to come back here. But now, he's happy there. It took him about a year.

Doreen: He calls me on Thursday night and says, "this is your son." And I say, "Oh really?" And he says, "Tomorrow's Friday; I'm coming home!" **Lance:** I'm coming home. **Doreen:** First thing, "Where's my chocolate milk?" "Yes, I have your milk and pizza." OK, he's happy. By Sunday, we can't get out of here fast enough. **Lance:** Yeah, I want to go back, all my buddies. **Doreen:** These photos are really old. One day I have to organize them. **Lance:** Mom, I want to look, I'm sitting down. **Doreen:** Lance, you land like an elephant sometimes. **Lance:** Oh, Mom don't call me a pest. **Doreen:** Well, you do pester. **Lance:** I don't pester so much anymore. **Doreen:** You're not a pest. I'd take my grand-kids for the weekend and Lance would get up in the middle of the night to help feed them. I said, "You don't have to get up if you hear me." But before I knew it he'd be in the room. He'd feed them. He'd play with them for hours on end. He has so much patience. He never showed any jealousy; sometimes I had to pay much more attention to them. He was so good with them. **Lance:** Oh, pictures of me, Mom. **Doreen:** Don't know why anyone would want pictures of you? **Lance:** You've got me Mom. **Doreen:** Yes, I know, I got you kiddo.

Jeff McNary

Sherry: I thought everybody had a brother like Jeff. But one day our parents talked to us. Nothing was secret in our house. No one knew that anything was wrong with Jeff until he was three months old. My mom had suspicions. She talked to the doctor and that's when they discovered he had brain damage. I don't know what they did, or how they knew. Jeffrey's case was simple. Maybe the umbilical cord was smashed or something and it kept him from getting any oxygen. There was no report from the doctor—that said he came out blue—there were no indicators. When I was in high school, Jeff went to the University of Washington and was part of a study on mental retardation. The only thing they could guess was oxygen deprivation at birth. It made me feel even sadder to think that before he was born he was normal—or OK. It wasn't an illness or a genetic thing. It was an accident and we don't know why. In those days no one came into the birthing room so there were no family members to be a witness. The mothers were sedated. Someone must have known that something went wrong.

My parents always stressed that we would have to look after him. When we were young, I thought Jeff could have an operation so he could talk. It took him a long time to walk. He would scoot and he fell down a lot, but finally he could walk. So I thought, now maybe he'll learn to talk. But, my parents explained how that was one of the major areas of his brain that had been damaged, and it wasn't really possible for him to learn to speak. I remember I became afraid, and wished he wasn't mentally retarded. This might sound strange but I remember thinking, what if I got some kind of illness and was going to die. I thought, I'd have to kill Jeff and then myself. I didn't trust society. Some people weren't really nice to us, even other families who had kids with a disability of some kind. Jeff was hyper and really too extreme in his behavior for other families to accept him. I was so afraid of the thought of him being left alone in the world.

When we were growing up Jeff got thrown out of a lot of things. He's kind of a teaser and full of mischievousness. He can light up the room with his smile and scream for joy about things he likes. But if he saw a mother scold a child he might go over and whack her. He wants everybody to be happy. He can sense when something's wrong. They said he had behavior problems. We were ostracized sometimes and that's when I got my distrust of society. I was in high school when the TV series *The Holocaust* was on and I learned that before they exterminated the Jews they exterminated people like Jeff. That terrified me. This might sound crazy, but I formulated a plan that if the Nazis or some other group should ever take over again, I was going to have my trunk full of camping tents, dried food, and sleeping bags ready. I'd take off with Jeff for the Canadian border and hike into the mountains and hide out there. I'm not sure if Jeff could realize an immediate danger, but I can tell when he's frightened.

Bob: Although he's retarded, he's actually pretty smart. Jeff's problem is that he understands everything we say and do, but we can't understand him. He'll con you into doing something for him, and if you don't know what he's talking about and you dare say yes—and then you don't do it—well, then he's mad. He doesn't realize that he's different than anyone else.

Myrtle: I don't know, he probably does. I'm not sure. Jeff's always happy about everything. He was very hyper as a child. He even had seizures. It wasn't epilepsy. It was just nerves. He loves people and he would grab them. I mean, in those days people didn't understand retardation. They were frightened, and they wouldn't want to be touched. Jeff does understand a lot. He watches TV, and looks at magazines, and goes to the movies. As the years went on he gradually got a little calmer, but he's still hyper.

Bob: We found with Jeff—when he was in town he was wild. I mean, you'd always have to hold his hand, so you couldn't do much. If we took him out to the woods or down to the ocean—where we had a mountain on one side and cold water on the other—we could let him run. So it was to our benefit to take him there. We got to like camping and backpacking. We still go.

Myrtle: When he was seven he was so hyper—we thought he should be in school at least part-time and we got him in the Central playschool. So we met other parents. Every family had a different problem because each child had a different problem. So you would learn from them, maybe you should try this, or maybe you should try that. And maybe it would help.

Bob: It started in 1963. We used to go down to Olympia a lot—the mother's mostly. And raise hell.

Myrtle: Yes, we'd go when bills were being discussed that might provide more money for the handicapped. If we wanted something, someone in the group would write up a proposal and present it. Through the mother's guilds we got as many people as possible to come. We had a calling committee. We would call people and bake a batch of cookies for a committee meeting at the same time. You just worked and ran after your kid and called people. I mean, it was chaos all the time. But it wasn't too hard to get people to attend things because within our group of parents our lives were so hard; we all agreed it had to be better. We just knew we had to do these things and we did them. We also hoped—once we did it—we would not have to worry and things would be smooth. But that's not the way it is. We are still battling and still hoping.

Bob: All the parents were afraid that when you got a program it wouldn't fit their child. After our meetings, some of the parents would go home crying and some would go fighting mad. Everyone was afraid that "My kid's going to be left out." The history of all these organizations was making a place for the retarded, but what happens is they find it's easier to work with some kids than it is for others. Always the kids that are harder to manage or more severely retarded get dropped out the bottom. It's like there's a class system of the handicapped. Our work was trying to find a place where that could never happen.

In every program there is always the worst kid and if

All through his school years and then in the sheltered workshop they said Jeff was very limited, and that his attention span would only last for about fifteen minutes. But they were wrong. We recently discovered he loved paper shredding. So I got him a contract with a company shredding. They expected that it would take him two or three years to finish the work. He finished the shredding in six months. Then I got him another job, and again they estimated that it would take him about six months. He did it in about a month. Jeffrey just plain loves to shred. He likes the cause and effect. He's very focused. He puts the paper in the shredder and it disappears. He likes the sound; and I think he likes the sense of accomplishment. We take bag after bag out of the shredder. He loves to see them pile up. One day I came in and he was patting his chest and pointing over to the pile of bags as if to say look what I did. I know he felt really good about himself, and that started at age forty-eight. Before that, I don't know if he ever had that sense of self-pride. It took a long time for Jeff to be allowed to do what he wanted to do. So now he's self-employed. When I go visit him in his office in

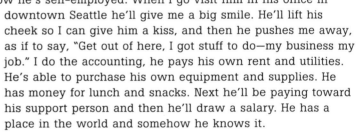

downtown Seattle he'll give me a big smile. He'll lift his cheek so I can give him a kiss, and then he pushes me away, as if to say, "Get out of here, I got stuff to do—my business my job." I do the accounting, he pays his own rent and utilities. He's able to purchase his own equipment and supplies. He has money for lunch and snacks. Next he'll be paying toward his support person and then he'll draw a salary. He has a place in the world and somehow he knows it.

STATE OF WASHINGTON

REGISTRATIONS

MASTER LIC

UNIFI

JEFFREY CALVIN MCNARY
DOC DESTRUCTION
21 2ND AVE
EATTLE WA 98104

ORGANIZATION TYPE
SOLE PROPRIETORSHIP

they threw him out your kid might be the second worse.

Sharon Gowdey

Dorothy, Dwight, and Sharon Gowdey

Dorothy: I didn't think I was going to have another child but we did. Sharon was born in 1963. I was forty-five. I was working on my art and painting as much as possible. I already had two little girls. Dr. Lee didn't want us to bring her home, he said it would be too hard to raise a child who had Down Syndrome. Our pediatrician said to take Sharon home and enjoy her. So we did. She had a little hole in her heart, but it healed. She's always been really healthy.

Dwight: We weren't told what to expect. I went to the library to find books on Down's and there was only one. At that time, they would say life expectancy was seventeen years, and we would probably have respiratory, heart, and numerous other problems. I gave the book to the pediatrician—he didn't know about it. Sharon developed very well. She walked fairly early—about fourteen or fifteen months. When she was born I had a medical policy through my profession. They covered the pregnancy but they wouldn't include her in the family plan because she was a "Mongoloid." After she was excluded I didn't carry any private health insurance. I checked a few other places and got the same answer. The first insurance she got is when she went to work.

Dwight: We both had been aware that for older people it was more probable to have a child with Down Syndrome, but the odds were pretty good so we thought we'd take a chance. We knew there might be a stigma attached to it, but there was really no alternative.

Dorothy: I don't remember that we knew about Down Syndrome, but it's true that in neighborhoods where handicapped children move in, they feel a reflected stigma. It's a sin of pride really—ly. Her sisters enjoyed her. In fact, she had three mothers. When she was little we read to her a lot, and she loves to read.

Dwight: I didn't know what else to do when she was quite young, particularily when she wasn't getting around the first year. I read to her and she seemed to like it. She started preschool at Northwest Center. Then Judge Utter, who also had a handicapped child, suggested we take her to the University of Washington to the CDMRC. She was with them for ten or twelve years. They did learning evaluations and they questioned that she really was a Down, she was so capable. So they gave her the genetic test. It was new at that time but it confirmed her condition.

Dorothy: She did so well they thought she might do better in a cooperative. When she went to Oaklake School the counselor said, "She'll have a harder time than anyone else because she's not severely retarded, yet she isn't normal. She's in between." It's the worse place you can be—because you don't fit in with the normal kids, like you would want to have a normal boyfriend and get married. Sometimes they made fun of her. She's close, but she doesn't quite make it. She likes people, she's always been gregarious. She works in the judicial system at the King County Courthouse. She files cases, does the recycling and the mail. It's a full-time job and she gets more than minimum wage and benefits.

Dwight: Soon after Sharon was born, I joined the ARC and a lot of other groups to try and learn things. I was often the only man in the group. But I'd been involved in politics so I was used to going to meetings. When I was vice president of the PTA I had an argument with one of the teachers. I wondered why Sharon didn't have homework. They had this attitude that these Special Ed students can't do it so don't bother. I saw a note he sent to the principal about that "pain-in-the-ass" Gowdey. I guess I got invovled more than most parents, but I think it was a way to adjust to the fact of Sharon's condition. We worked it in with the rest of our lives, as you do with any other child. You do what's necessary.

99

Sharon & Dad

Sharon's Family
Smiled at 3 mo.
Laughed at 5 mo.
6 Mo. old
Sharon can turn over - is
trying to crawl - Holds her
head up well - Will wipe her
face when asked - Has been
kissing us since she was
2½ - She can pick up a pill.
Knows how to handle a
spoon fairly well. Still nurses
but refuses a bottle, drinks extra milk from a glass - Sleeps from 7:30 - 6 AM.

Dec. 1963

Dorothy: I couldn't paint for a while after Sharon was born, but that was OK, I'd rather have Sharon than that. We hadn't been around handicapped children before. It's nice to know about them.

Dwight: Sharon has always had a good opinion of herself. When she was young my prayer was that she would grow up and live a normal life. In everything except her social life, I think she is doing very normal.

Sharon: I'm half Down's and half normal. We are all human actually, but with Down Syndrome we are different. I have one chromosome in me and that means . . . well the doctor took one look at me. I was born wrong so to speak. They thought they made a mistake. I'm half Down's and that means I'm mosaic. It's not easy to have Down's; to me it's confusing actually. I don't know why. Sometimes I confuse myself. I'm happy. I'm happy to have a family that supports me. . . .

I was in the Special Olympics first in '76. I won a lot of ribbons and medals. I kept winning. I didn't lose very much. Losing is not very good. Winning is. Winners never quit! I know that. It was pretty hard. Sometimes I thought I might not win. I don't think about that any more—I only think about winning.

Collage by Dorothy Gowdey

Sharon: I don't have pictures of me at work. They won't let me, no, not in the courthouse. They don't allow cameras in the courthouse. I feel comfortable at work sometimes, but there were two scary times actually. The year I came in was 1999 and the WTO was happening, so it was hard to get into the courthouse. The other time was the earthquake. It was pretty scary. The place rumbled all right! We had to run and hide under our table.

You can take a picture of my desk, but it's pretty messy. I've lived here all my life, since I was born. I might someday get my own apartment. It might take a while, but who knows. It would be interesting. It would be kind of fun. My apartment would have a hot tub. Ha, you bet. It would have a kitchen, a deck, um, a living room, an eating room, a bedroom, closet space, hee hee. I'd have plates and stuff in the kitchen and a microwave. I actually don't know yet what my plates would look like— let's see, off white with little flowers—and I'd have carpets and rugs. I might get a roommate; I mean it's possible . . .

I mean, it's possible . . .

Acknowledgments

I would like to deeply thank Kathi Whittaker and Nancy Meltzer, the founding members of the Seattle Family Network who initially conceived the idea for a project—"to tell the stories of our senior families"—and wrote a proposal to Seattle's Office of Arts & Cultural Affairs. Longtime friends of one another they have both worked for many years as advocates for their own children, Matthew and Adam, as well as being tireless activists in disability politics. Kathi took on the principal role as project coordinator and faithfully held together all of the project's multiple threads as it meandered and grew. Her openness and gentle patience were greatly appreciated. Together they kept me on track to realize the envisioned goal. I would also like to thank the other steadfast members of the Seattle Family Network: Sherry McNary, Bill Sellars, Delia Cano, Harriet Sanderson, and Fran Elliot, who contributed many hours and stories and so carefully introduced me to the world of disability politics. I would like to extend an extra thanks to Sherry McNary for her hospitality and our many evening discussions, and to Harriet Sanderson, an accomplished artist who generously contributed her creative time as well as often acted as "artist translator." Thanks also goes to Venus Bravo De Rueda for joining and helping to guide our group during its last year of planning.

As this project grew from an artist-produced venture to a published book I depended upon the advice and help of numerous friends and professional colleagues. I would like to thank Diane Burk for collaborating with me on the design and feel of the book. She took a rather chaotic image and text layout and developed it into an integrated whole. I would also like to thank Melissa Alexander for reading and commenting on the text, giving advice on the selections of photographs, and for developing the first outline for the timeline from an unruly pile of collected notes. I would also like to thank Linda Dackman for translation services and Ellen Hament, for her first-hand knowledge of the disability experience and for editing the first manuscript. Kurt Fleichtmeir and Stephen Vincent gave me valuable advice in my search for a publisher and Douglas Harper looked at an early manuscript and recommended I bring it to the attention of University of Washington Press.

I would also like to thank the many readers and advisors who generously read and commented on the book and gave me the encouragement and confidence to continue: Paul Longmore, David Wellman, Steve Eidelman, Louise Victor, Bill Cirocco, Dennis Lang, Jim Whittaker, Sherrie Brown, Kurt Johnson, Larry Jones, and Gail Dubrow. Thanks also goes to Tim Waters, Ira Nowinski, Debra Lehtone, Rupert Jenkins, Rebecca Solnit, Charlie Schwartzenberg, Amy Tracktenberg, Ann Worthington, and Elliot Ross for discussing the many themes and ideas this book generated.

A very special thanks also goes to the Office of Arts & Cultural Affairs and the guidance of Barbara Goldstein and Lisa Richmond. Their design of the program, Artist Residencies Transforming Urban Places, em-bodied the idea that by investing in artists and believing in their intuitive processes, creative contributions can be made to the greater society—often in unpredictable ways. It was indeed an honor to participate in the program. I would especially like to thank Lisa Richmond as Director of ARTSUP for her advice and patience as *Becoming Citizens* evolved. An additional thanks also goes to the ARC of King County, Senior Family Caregiver Support Project for their generous support.

I would also like to thank Jeffrey McNary, Lupita Cano, Matthew Whittaker, Kari Sellars, and Adam Meltzer for letting me participate in little pieces of their lives.

This project was also about acknowledging the ways people influence one another to make necessary social and political change happen. With this in mind I would like to acknowledge, and thank, Merrill Nelson, Patrick Dolan, Martha Armour (Pym), Stella Safioles, Aaron Werner, Naida Taggart, Marie Strausbaugh, Sharon Gowdey, Lance Peake, David Bass, Jeffrey McNary, Coolidge Chapman, Mike Hiramatsu, and their families and also Rodney and Cheryl Wilson and their family.

I also was very inspired by and want to humbly acknowledge the work of the Education for All Committee: Cecile Lindquist, Janet Taggart, Katie Dolan, Evelyn Chapman, and William Dussault. Their painstaking work in ensuring that the Education for All Handicapped Children Act passed, and their continuing work in both the local and national community is tireless. They acted both as story participants and as project guideposts. They introduced me to the ins and outs of community politics and suffered through many "let's remember back" evenings. Their intelligence, determination, and humor are indeed remarkable.

I would like to also thank Pat Soden and Jacquie Ettinger of the University of Washington Press for their guidance, support, and encouragement as the manuscript became finalized.

This book is dedicated to the anonymous—those who daily change the world by imagining alternative futures.

—Susan Schwartzenberg

STATE OF WASHINGTON
OFFICE OF THE GOVERNOR

OLYMPIA

DANIEL J. EVANS
GOVERNOR

May 18, 1971

Cecile Lindquist
2526 N. E. 106th Place
Seattle, Washington   98125

Dear Cecile:

I want to personally thank and commend you for your work on House Bill 90
and Senate Bill 66. It is extremely pleasing to me to know that all
handicapped children will now receive an education in the public schools.
I believe it is safe to say that House Bille 90 is the most significant
mental retardation law to pass in the history of Washington State.

The Education for All Committee could disband now with their original goals
accomplished, but I urge you to continue your work. Adequate funding must
be provided from future Legislative sessions, the causes of mental retardation must be found and eliminated, institutionalization of children must
come to a close as community concepts develop and finally every retarded
and handicapped person must be represented in the courts, agencies and
communities of this land.

You have led the way and should continue to do so.

Sincerely,

Daniel J. Evans
Governor

DJE/cjd
Enclosure

Afterword

Becoming Citizens is a remarkable collection of stories about a special group of pioneering family advocates in Washington State who made waves—creating the conditions that would have a profound effect on the lives of their own special-needs children and many others to follow. If you have been involved in developmental disabilities in any way, as a family member, volunteer, neighbor, professional, or public official, you will recognize the stories and the people in them. Regardless of where families lived, the stories are the same. Here they are told in a way that will capture your heart—even if you have never thought about children with disabilities before in your life.

Being the parents of a child with a disability is not a spectator sport. If your child does not have a disability our society provides the structure, the institutions, the systems for raising him or her to adulthood: from childcare to school, to health care, to civic institutions like scouts, sports leagues, drama clubs, and religious and cultural institutions, American society was and is structured, albeit imperfectly, to provide the support and framework for successful adulthood. Not so for children and families who live with disability. Political and policy involvement for families without a child with a disability is optional: important, but not mandatory. If your child has a disability, it isn't optional. As one of the leaders of the disability movement, the late Justin Dart, Jr. often said, "Be involved with politics as if your life depended on it . . . because it does." Justin would have loved this book. He would have recognized these stories.

Being politically naïve and apathetic is not an option for parents of sons and daughters with cognitive disabilities such as mental retardation, whether those sons and daughters are children at home or adults in their own communities. Perhaps one of the biggest changes to emerge since these families took the first brave steps is that people with serious, lifelong disabilities such as mental retardation are, for the first time in the history of the world, living to old age. They are outliving their parents and, at the same time, becoming part of the greying of America, an America that is not ready for them to this day.

Many of Washington's families experienced what was the norm at the time—told by doctors to not take their children home from the hospital, to forget about them, they would damage your family, harm your other children's development. Unlike today, professionals then were often "the enemy"—they ignored or diminished these sons and daughters at the same time the social, cultural, and religious systems were, by and large, ignoring and rejecting them as well. Thanks to these pioneering families there are, today, hundreds of training programs for professionals in all imaginable disciplines. Where parents are faculty, disability is considered a natural part of the human condition, and undergraduate, graduate, and postgraduate students are taught how to support and include people, not how to label and exclude them. The professions are better for it as well.

Others experienced kind and helpful physicians, educators, social workers, and clergy, and got what support was available. Some were inspired by these same healers to do more for their child and then for others.

Many families got together to start schools, special classes in school or church basements or in vacant storefronts. They raised money through raffles, bake sales, and philanthropy to get their child the social goods provided easily to their fellow citizens, benefits that other children and families took for granted: a free public education; the chance to get a job, a shot at their piece of the American Dream. When you read these stories, these tales of struggle and accomplishment, you will see some bitterness and disappointment. But what you will see most clearly is the strength of character of American families. Not those families who make headlines, not those who you think of as thought leaders. These are ordinary families made extraordinary through their struggles and accomplishments.

In the life narratives and photos that make up *Becoming Citizens*, we hear the full range of emotions: the anger, sadness, and pride expressed by these families. Anger at society for rejecting and neglecting their children, sadness at not being able to do more, and pride at what their children had become, what working together they could accomplish

Many of these stories take place in parallel with other more visible trends and changes in American society—the women's movement, the civil rights movement, the movements to accept other groups defined as different into the mainstream of American society. Given all of these movements, America today is better for the struggle. The struggle for the rights and opportunities of people with disabilities and their families is at least as powerful as the others, and perhaps more so because the struggle was done mostly outside of the limelight, behind the scenes. The gains made since World War II would not have been possible without the support of elected officials at the local, county, state, and national level. Most of them, like these pioneering Washington State family advocates, never got public credit for what they did. We thank them now.

Every elected official, civil servant, educator, legal and helping professional, and member of the clergy should read these stories. It will make them better at what they do, and make our nation stronger. *Becoming Citizens* honors those parents whose efforts changed past conditions, helped create the present, and laid both the statutory and inspirational foundation for the future. We are in their debt.

—Steve Eidelman, Executive Director of
    The Arc of the United States

Glossary

ADA Public Law 101-336—Americans with Disabilities Act, enacted July 26, 1990; prohibits discrimination and ensures equal opportunity in employment, state and local government services, public accommodations, commercial facilities, and transportation. It also mandates the establishment of TDD/telephone relay services.

ARC—refers to the ARC of King County (started in 1936 as CBL, see below), which has been a leader in the development of services and programs for people with developmental disabilities and their families; affiliated with ARC of Washington State and ARC of the United States.

Autism—a neurological disorder that affects an individual's ability to communicate, understand language, play, and relate to others (National Dissemination Center for Children with Disabilities).

B. F. Day (Benjamin Franklin Day)—a public elementary school in Seattle; a site for preschool children with disabilities from the Seattle area.

Boeing Employees Good Neighbor Fund—employee-contributed funds used to make grants to non-profit organizations, tailored to the needs of the local community.

Brown vs. Board of Education—U.S. Supreme Court decision in 1954 to outlaw "separate but equal" education resulting in desegregation of schools.

CBL—In 1936, a group of parents whose children were living in institutions formed the Children's Benevolent League of Washington (CBL), now known as the ARC of Washington State. Initially, members focused their efforts on improving the conditions and treatment of individuals residing in the state's only institution for people with disabilities.

CDMRC—Child Development Mental Retardation Center at the University of Washington, now called Tthe Center for Human Development and Disability (CHDD); makes important contributions to the lives of people with developmental disabilities and their families through a comprehensive array of research, clinical services, training, community outreach, and dissemination activities (from CHDD Web site).

Central School—a primary school started by parents of children with developmental disabilities located in the basement of Temple De Hirsch, later merged with other parent-run schools to form Northwest Center.

Cerebral palsy—a term used to describe a group of chronic conditions affecting body movement and muscle coordination caused by damage to one or more areas of the brain before, during, or after birth.

Children's—refers to Children's Orthopedic Hospital, now called Children's Hospital and Regional Medical Center; a pediatric hospital and teaching site for the University of Washington School of Medicine in Seattle.

Cognitive disablity—A disability that impacts an individual's ability to access, process, or remember information. (The Center on Human Policy at Syracuse University)

Developmental Disabilities Act since 1963—the Developmental Disabilities Assistance and Bill of Rights Act has made a crucial difference in the lives and futures of individuals with developmental disabilities and their families. Through this Act, federal funds support the development and operation of state councils, protection and advocacy systems, university centers (formerly known as university affiliated programs), and projects of national significance (see CDMRC, a university center).

Developmental Disability—There are nearly four million Americans with developmental disabilities. Developmental disabilities are severe, chronic disabilities attributable to mental and/or physical impairment, which manifest before age twenty two and are likely to continue indefinitely. They result in substantial limitations in three or more areas: self-care, receptive and expressive language, learning, mobility, self-direction, capacity for independent living, and economic self-sufficiency, as well as the continuous need for individually planned and coordinated services. (from Adminstration on Developmental Disabilities, U.S. Department of Health and Human Services. ADD)

Down Syndrome—Down Syndrome is a genetic condition that causes delays in physical and intellectual development. It occurs in approximately one in every 800 live births. Individuals with Down Syndrome have 47 chromosomes instead of the usual 46. It is the most frequently occurring chromosonal disorder. Down Syndrome is not related to race, nationality, religion or socioeconomic status. the most important fact to know about individuals with Down Syndrome is that they are more like others than different. (National Association for Down Syndrome)

Epton funds—refers to the 1962 Kathryn Epton Bill that provided funds to pay for the care of those children on the waiting list for state institutions for developmentally disabled individuals.

Epilepsy—Epilepsy is a brain disorder in which clusters of nerve cells, or neurons, in the brain sometimes signal abnormally. In epilepsy, the normal pattern of neuronal activity becomes disturbed, causing strange sensations, emotions, and behavior or sometimes convulsions, muscle spasms, and loss of consciousness. Epilepsy is a disorder with many possible causes. Anything that disturbs the normal pattern of neuron activity—from illness to brain damage to abnormal brain development—can lead to seizures. Epilepsy may develop because of an abnormality in brain wiring, an imbalance of nerve signaling chemicals called neurotransmitters, or some combination of these factors.(National Institute of Neurological Disorders and Stroke. NINDS)

Eugenics—the study of ways in which the physical and mental quality of a people can be controlled and improved by selective breeding, and the belief that this should be done. (Webster New World Encyclopedia 1992.

Fircrest School—established in 1959 and certified as an IMR (Institution for the Mentally Retarded) in 1978; occupies a campus of approximately 80 acres. At its peak it served between 1,000 and 1,200 residents; presently 214 individuals reside there (6/04). Fircrest serves individuals with a variety of developmental disabilities, but has always had a focus on providing care for people with extreme physical challenges.

Foundation for Handicapped Children—organization formed to support people with developmental disabilities by overseeing their welfare after death of family members.

Fourteenth Amendment—ratified in 1868. Section 1. All persons born or naturalized in the United States, and subject to the jurisdiction thereof, are citizens of the United States and of the state wherein they reside. No state shall make or enforce any law which shall abridge the privileges or immunities of citizens of the United States; nor shall any state deprive any person of life, liberty, or property, without due process of law; nor deny to any person within its jurisdiction the equal protection of the laws.

Gardner, Howard—Harvard psychologist who developed the theory of multiple intelligence.

Early Head Start—a free childhood program for pregnant women and children from birth to age five. The goal of these programs is to help children from low-income families get a healthy start and become ready for school. Both programs give children and their families a wide range of educational and social services. Head Start is a free pre-school program for three–five year-old children from low-income families. Early Head Start serves pregnant women, infants, and toddlers.

Hopecrest School—one of the early programs for children with disabilities in Seattle before public school access; later merged to form Northwest Center.

House Bill 90—Washington State Education for All Bill passed in 1971.

IEP—Individualized Education Program—a child receiving special education services under IDEA must have an IEP; a written document, created by a team of educators and their parents, describing the educational goals for the school year, as well as any special supports that are needed to help achieve those goals.

IDEA—Individuals with Disabilities Education Act; the reauthorization and renaming of the Education for All Handicapped Children Act; 1990. The federal law that underpins most special education services in the country.

Inquiry based learning—focuses on using and learning content as a means to develop information-processing and problem-solving skills.

League of Women Voters—a nonpartisan political organization that encourages the informed and active participation of citizens in government, works to increase understanding of major public policy issues, and influences public policy through education and advocacy.

Lowell School—a Seattle elementary public school that provides some programs for children with disabilities.

Mental Retardation—Mental retardation is characterized both by a significantly below-average score on a test of mental ability or intelligence and by limitations in the ability to function in areas of daily life, such as communication, self-care, and getting along in social situations and school activities. Mental retardation is sometimes referred to as a cognitive or intellectual disability. Children with mental retardation can and do learn new skills, but they develop more slowly than children with average intelligence and adaptive skills. There are different degrees of mental retardation, ranging from mild to profound. A person's level of mental retardation can be defined by their intelligence quotient (IQ), or by the types and amount of support they need (National Center on Birth Defects and Developmental Disabilities)

Mills vs. Board of education—1972—rules that disabled children cannot be barred from public schools.

Mongoloid—archaic term used for the condition of Down Syndrome; now viewed as a negative term by individuals with disabilities and their families.

Nellie Goodhue School—for handicapped children, a segregated school run by Seattle Public Schools. Nellie Goodhue was an early educator of children with disabilities.

Normalization Movement—a philosophy that promotes the provision of services and supports to people with disabilities in ways that are most typically provided in society for people without disabilities.

Northwest Center for the Retarded—an organization founded by parents in 1965 to provide education programs for children and work training programs for adults.

Oaklake School—a Seattle elementary public school that provided some special education classes for children with disabilities.

Pacific School—refers to Wilson Pacific School, a Seattle high school education and vocational program for students with developmental disabilities and other special education students.

Parc v. Pennsylvania—1971—(PARC: Pennsylvania Association of Retarded Children) strikes a state law prohibiting disabled children from attending public schools.

People First—a self-advocacy organization started by and for people with developmental disabilities. It began in 1974 at a national conference on Developmental Disabilities in Oregon. Over 600 people with disabilities attended the conference; by its end a new organization was formed. Initiated and run by persons with disabilities, this organization has many goals—inclusion in society, jobs, housing, closing institutions, creating legislation to prevent abuse in group homes, and other public and private institutions.

Public Law 94.142 Free Appropriate Education—federal Education for All Handicapped Children Act of 1975.

Rehabilitation Act Section 504—a civil rights law that prohibits discrimination on the basis of disability. This law applies to, among other entities, public elementary and secondary schools. Children with disabilities may be eligible for special education and related services under Section 504 of the Rehabilitation Act of 1973, as amended. (NICHCY)

Ritalin—medication used to treat hyperactivity in children and adults

Seattle Parks Department program—provided recreation programs for the citizens of Seattle and in 1966 created a program for children with disabilities

Section 8—a federally funded housing subsidy program that provides low-income individuals or families the opportunity to choose and lease safe, decent, and affordable privately owned rental housing by supplementing what they could afford on their own.

Seguin School—Seattle private special education primary school for children. Utilized methods developed by early educational theorist Eduard Seguin.

Spastic Children's Preschool and Clinic—currently known as Boyer Children's Clinic in Seattle; established in 1949; provided early intervention services for very young children with cerebral palsy and other disabilities.

Sudden Infant Death—a diagnosis given for the sudden death of an infant under the age of one year that remains unexplained after a complete investigation

Title XIX—amendment to the Social Security Act that established Medicaid services, and which funds health care and long-term care services for people on Supplemental Security Income.

Troubleshooters—a statewide protection and advocacy program for people with developmental disabilities and their families started in 1972 by parents. Later became the Washington Protection and Advocacy System.

Wolfensberger, Dr. Wolf—spearheaded the "normalization" reform movement in the USA and Canada in 1972.

WTO—refers to the 1999 World Trade Organization meeting held in Seattle that was protested by antiglobalization activists.

Bibliography

Disability Studies, History and Theory

Fleischer, Doris Zames and Zames, Frieda, *The Disability Rights Movement: From Charity to Confrontation.* Philadelphia: Temple University Press, 2001

Goffman, Irving, *Stigma: Notes on the Management of Spoiled Identity.* New York: Simon & Schuster Inc., 1963

Ingstad, Benedicte, and Whyte, Susan Reynolds, *Disability and Culture.* Berkeley, University of California Press, 1995

Linton, Simi, *Claiming Disability: Knowledge and Identity.* New York: New York University Press, 1998

Longmore, Paul K., and Umansky, Lauri, *The New Disability History, American Perspectives.* New York: New York University Press, 2001

Longmore, Paul K., *Why I Burned My Book and Other Essays on Disability.* Philadelphia: Temple University Press, 2003

Meyer, Donald, and Vadasy, Patricia, *Living with a Brother or Sister with Special Needs: A Book for Sibs.* Seattle: University of Washington Press, 2000

Noll, Steven, and Trent, James W. Jr., *Mental Retardation in America: A Historical Reader.* New York: New York University Press, 2004

Parallels In Time, a cd and website, http://www.mncdd.org/parallels/menu.html, The Minnesota Governor's Council on Developmental Disabilities, 1996

Trent, James W. Jr., *Inventing the Feeble Mind: A History of Mental Retardation in America.* Berkeley: University of California Press, 1994

Turnbull, H.R., and Turnbull, Ann P., *Parents Speak Out: Then and Now.* Columbus: Charles E. Merrill Publishing, 1985

Institutions and Hospitals

Blatt, Burton, and Kaplan, Fred, *Christmas in Purgatory: A Photographic Essay on Mental Retardation.* Syracuse: Human Policy Press, 1974

Foucault, Michel, *Madness and Civilization: A History of Insanity in the Age of Reason.* New York: Random House, 1965

Foucault, Michel, *The Birth of the Clinic: An Archeology of Medical Perception.* New York: Pantheon Books, 1973

Goffman, Irving, *Asylums: Essays on the Social Situation of Mental Patients and other Inmates.* New York: Anchor/Doubleday Books, 1961

Risse, Guenter B., *Mending Bodies, Saving Souls: A History of Hospitals.* New York: Oxford University Press, 1999

Wolfensberger, Wolf, *The Origin and Nature of Our Institutional Models.* Syracuse: Human Policy Press, 1975

Eugenics

Carlson, Elof Axel, *The Unfit: A History of a Bad Idea.* Cold Spring Harbor: Cold Spring Harbor Laboratory Press, 2001

Eugenics Record Office, Cold Spring Harbor Laboratory Archives website, http://nucleus.cshl.org/CSHLlib/ , documents, photographs and records of the Eugenics record office under the Direction of Dr. Charles B. Davenport, 1910-21.

Gould, Stephen J., *The Mismeasure of Man.* New York: W. W. Norton and Co., 1996

Kline, Wendy, *Building a Better Race: Gender, Sexuality, and Eugenics from the Turn of the Century to the Baby Boom.* Berkeley: University of California Press, 2001

Kevles, Daniel J., *In the Name of Eugenics: Genetics and the Uses of Human Heredity.* Cambridge: Harvard University Press, 1985

History, Activism, and Citizenship

Rabben, Linda, *Fierce Legion of Friends: A History of Human Rights Campaigns and Campaigners.* Brentwood: Quixote Center, 2002

Rousseau, Jean Jacques, *The Social Contract, Or principles of Political Right,* http://www.constitution.org/jjr/socon.htm, The Constitution Society, originally published 1762

Schama, Simon, *Citizens: A Chronicle of the French Revolution.* New York: Vintage Books/Random House, 1989

Zinn, Howard, *A People's History of the United States.* New York: Harper Collins Publishing, 1980

Washington State History

Brecheen, Barbara, *Developmental Disabilities Services: An Historical Outline, 1861-1980.* Olympia: Publication of the Division of Developmental Disabilities, 2000

Hollander, Russell, *Our Brothers' Keepers: The Story of Human Services in Washington, 1853-1932. Columbia* Spring 1989

Jones, Larry A., and Barnes, Phyllis A., *Doing Justice: A History of the Association for Retarded Citizens of Washington.* Olympia: ARC of Washington, 1987

Schwartz, Susan, *Fuller Lives for the Retarded—A Continuing Struggle. The Seattle Times,* Sunday, March 20, 1977

Taggart, Janet, and Head, Barry, *Time to Make a Bold New Start,* The Retarded Part II, (undated article from the personal collection of Janet Taggart)

Whelan, Howard J. Jr., *With Love and Homemade Bread.* Unpublished draft for article, 1980

Education

Howe, Samuel Gridley, "Report Made to the Legislature of Massachusetts,1848." Reprinted in Trent, James W., *Inventing the Feeble Mind: A History of Mental Retardation in America.* Berkeley: University of California Press, 1994, pp. 23–26

Lane, Harlan, *The Wild Boy of Aveyron.* Cambridge: Harvard University Press, 1976

Locke, John, *An Essay Concerning Human Understanding.* London: Penguin Books, 1997, first published 1689

Mondale, Sarah, and Patton, Sarah B., *School: The Story of American Public Education* (companion book to PBS series of same title). Boston: Beacon Press, 2001

Stories and Case Studies

Buck, Pearl S., *The Child Who Never Grew.* New York: John Day, 1950

Featherstone, Helen, *A Difference in the Family: living with a Disabled Child.* London/New York: Penguin Books, 1980

Folkenflik, Robert, *The Culture of Autobiography: Constructions of Self Representation.* Stanford: Stanford University Press, 1993

Hart, Charles, *Without Reason: A Family Copes with Two Generations of Autism.* New York: Harper and Rowe, 1989

McHugh, Mary, *Special Siblings: Growing Up with Someone with a Disability.* Baltimore: Paul H. Brooks Publishing, 2003

Nolan, Christopher, *Under the Eye of the Clock: The Life Story of Christopher Nolan.* New York: St. Martin's Press, 1987

Rogers, Dale Evans, *Angel Unaware.* Grand Rapids: Fleming H. Revell/Baker Book House Co., 1953

Sacks, Oliver, *An Anthropologist on Mars,* New York: Alfred A. Knopf, 1995

Photography and Representation

Barthes, Roland, *Camera Lucida: Reflections on Photography.* New York: Hill and Wang, 1981

Berger, John, and Mohr, John, *Another Way of Telling.* New York: Random House, 1982

Collier, John Jr., and Collier, Malcolm, *Visual Anthropology: Photography as a Research Method.* New Mexico: University of New Mexico Press, 1986

Lesy, Michael, *Time Frames: The Meaning of Family Pictures.* New York: Pantheon Books, 1980

Smith, Shawn Michelle, *American Archives: Gender, Race, and Class in Visual Culture.* Princeton: Princeton University Press, 1999

Sontag, Susan, *On Photography.* New York: Farrar, Straus and Giroux, 1977

Spence, Jo, and Holland, Patricia, *Family Snaps: The Meanings of Domestic Photography.* London: Virago Press Limited, 1991.

Stange, Maren, *Social Documentary Photography in America, 1890-1950.* Cambridge: Cambridge University Press, 1989

Thomson, Rosemarie Garland, *Freakery: Cultural Spectacles of the Extraordinary Body.* New York: New York University Press, 1996

Timeline

"I think I am something, I am, I exist."
1642 Meditations, René Descartes.

1690 *An Essay Concerning Human Understanding*, John Locke.

1693 *Thoughts Concerning Education*, John Locke

1722 Connecticut builds a house of correction. Inmates include people who are "mentally afflicted."

1735 *Systema Naturae*, Carolus Linnaeus.

1754 *Discourse on the Inequalities of Men*, Jean Jacques Rousseau.

1754 *Traité des Sensations*, Étienne Bonnot de Condillac. Human faculties originate from sensations.

1762 *The Social Contract*, Jean Jacques Rousseau.

1762 *Émile*, Jean Jacques Rousseau—novel on the ideals of education—knowledge is built from the individual.

1765 *Encyclopédie* published.

1776 U.S. Declaration of Independence, Thomas Jefferson.

1778 Thomas Jefferson calls for a two-tiered public education system.

1784 Philippe Pinel, a doctor acquainted with the philosophy of Locke, writes a series of articles about hygiene and mental disorders while the editor of the *Gazette de Santé*.

1788 U.S.Constitution ratified.

1789 Parisians storm the Bastille.

1789 Emmanuel Sieyes—Declaration of the Rights of Man and Citizens—Preamble to French Constitution.

1790 U.S. Naturalization Act, limits citizenship to free white persons.

1791 Bill of Rights—First 10 Amendments to the Constitution.

1791 The Rights of Man, Thomas Paine.

1791 *Medical and Philosophical Treatise on Insanity*, Philippe Pinel.

1793 Reign of Terror—Committee of Public Safety; Paris under Robespierre.

1793 Pinel releases "insane" inmates of the Bicetré Hospital from their shackles and cells.

1795 Pinel becomes chief physician of Hospice de la Salpêtrière, which includes a 600-bed ward for the mentally ill. He is considered

responsible for the overturn of the idea that mental illness was demonic possession and was a proponent of "Moral Therapy"—the idea of treating the mentally ill humanely. Ideas related to the French Revolution.

1797 Victor, the wild boy of Aveyron, who is considered to be the first documented case of autism, is captured in the woods near Lacaune, France.

1797 Phrenology is introduced by Francis Gall as a science of the mind.

1798 *The Principles of Population*, Malthus—population grows faster than food supply—argues for population control

1800 English "poorhouses" are adopted—to handle massive influx of people coming into cities for work. This included people who were "inconvenient" or "inadequate." People who couldn't work, were ill, disabled, or stood in the way of progress.

1801 Jean Itard, considered by some to be "the father of special education," begins teaching and documenting the life and development of Victor—the wild boy of Aveyron. Earliest demonstration that a person with a developmental disability can learn.

1817 Thomas Gallaudet and Laurent Clerc establish the Connecticut Asylum for the Education and Instruction of Deaf and Dumb Persons.

1820 Mentally afflicted individuals are sold at auction to the lowest bidder or given to those willing to take financial responsibility for them.

1820 The first public high school opens in America.

1827 Massachusetts passes a law making public school open to all students free of charge.

1829 Louis Braille invents a raised alphabet system that can be used by the blind to read.

1830 Due to the work of Horace Mann a statewide school system of common schools begins to emerge, paid for by property tax.

1836 *Nature*, Ralph Waldo Emerson.

1839 First Common School law enacted.

1839 Eduard Seguin and Jean-Etienne Esquirol publish a treatise summarizing their efforts to educate an "idiot" boy. Esquirol categorizes forms of mental retardation. He is a doctor and phrenologist.

1840 Eduard Seguin appointed head teacher of "idiot" children at Salpêtrière.

1840 American census measures extent of insanity and idiocy.

1840 The U.S. sees sharp rise in immigration. Education is promoted as a deterrent to crime.

1841 Dorthea Dix begins advocating for better services for people with disabilities and mental illness.

1842 P. T. Barnum begins exhibiting people he calls "freaks" in New York City.

1844 *Self Reliance*, Ralph Waldo Emerson

1846 Northern blacks in Boston petition the Boston School Committee to end the city's segregation policy.

1846 Seguin publishes *Traitment Moral: Hygiene, et Education des Idiots*. Drawing on theories of Locke and Condillac, Seguin developed the technique he called physiological education. Starting with the senses as a way to develop the mind, teachers could expose students to notions to stir their curiosity, but on their own they must explore for themselves. He emphasized active involvement of pupils. His methods went against formal instruction techniques: Memorization, non-active book-learning. "Away with the books. Seeing and feeling all at once—promotes understanding".

1847 "Report to the Legislature of Massachusetts", Samuel Gridley Howe.

1847 Samuel Gridley Howe starts the first publicly funded residential institution for the feebleminded in Massachusetts.

1848 Howe is influenced by the work of Pinel and Seguin and the idea that moral treatment in educational practices for "idiot" children will make them productive members of society. Schools for "feebleminded-improvables" begin to open.

1848 Sarah Roberts is barred from a local primary school in Boston because she is black and her father sues the city, beginning the separate but equal debate in America.

1850 Eduard Seguin emigrates to U.S. and works briefly with Samuel Gridley Howe.
"Not to teach this or that but to develop human function"—Seguin.

1850 Over 1 million Irish immigrants settle in U.S.

1851 Education becomes compulsory in Massachusetts.

1854 In Syracuse, New York, the first institution for the "feebleminded" is built.

1855 A law banning segregation in Massachusetts's schools is passed.

1857 Economic panic causes high unemployment.

1858 Charles Darwin publishes *The Origin of Species*.

1860 Herbert Spencer coins the term "Survival of the Fittest," minting the idea of Social Darwinism.

1863 The Emancipation Proclamation, Abraham Lincoln.

1864 Enabling Act, Columbia Institution for the Deaf and Dumb and Blind is given authority to give college degrees, signed by Abraham Lincoln. This is the first college in the world expressly established for people with disabilities.

1865 Four million slaves are freed in the United States.

1865 Thirteenth Amendment—prohibits slavery.

1865 Gregor Mendel presents paper on inheritance patterns in peas.

1866 Samuel Gridley Howe gives speech about caring for imperfect children. He believes higher numbers of "idiot children" are born to immigrants and the lower classes.

1868 Fourteenth Amendment ratified. Defines U.S. citizenship. It forbids any state to deny to any person "life, liberty, or property, without due process of law" or to "deny to any person within its jurisdiction the equal protection of its laws."

1870 "In the race of life where an individual is backward or peculiar and attempts to compete . . . the disadvantages are so great that the graduate from the idiot school cannot succeed." —C. T. Wilbur. "Schools for the Feebleminded" gradually become custodial asylums.

1872 *The Expression of Emotions in Man and Animals* is published by Charles Darwin.

1876 In *The Delinquent Man*, Cesare Lambroso used Darwin's theories to account for criminal behavior.

1877 The withdrawal of troops from the South as Reconstruction begins.

1883 "Eugenics" as a field of inquiry is coined by Francis Galton, a British photographer and cousin of Charles Darwin. Eugenics—Greek for good in birth.

1884 *Origins of the Family, Private Property, and the State,* by Frederick Engels.

1896 Massachusetts legally permits segregation in schools.

1896 Plessy versus Ferguson—Segregation and separate but equal becomes constitutionally legal.

1903 *The Story of My Life*, Helen Keller.

1905 Supreme Court requires California to extend public education to the children of Chinese immigrants.

1907 Indiana becomes the first state to enact laws to sterilize those deemed or classified as "hopeless or imbeciles."

1909 NAACP is formed.

1911 Charles Davenport publishes *Trait Book*, a study of behavioral traits, while Director of Cold Spring Harbor Biological laboratory where he established the Eugenics Records Office.

1911 Congress passes a joint resolution authorizing the appointment of a federal commission to investigate the idea of workers' compensation and the liability of employers for financial compensation to disabled workers.

1912 The book *The Kallikak Family,* by Henry H. Goddard, is published, proposing that disability is linked to immorality.

1913 21 states have established Worker's Compensation programs after progressive activists campaign for benefits.

1915 Dr. Harry J. Haiselden begins a crusade opposing surgery for babies born "defective" and is brought to court in Chicago when he allows a baby to starve to death because it is born deformed due to its mother contracting typhoid fever during pregnancy.

1916 Eugenics Record Office produces intelligence tests for men inducted in the military and encourages sterilization for the "unfit." Eugenics campaigns against people of color and immigrants lead to passage of "Jim Crow" laws in the South and legislation restricting immigration by Southern and Eastern Europeans, Asians, Africans, and Jews.

1917 Smith-Hughs Veteran Vocational Education Act.

1918 The Smith-Sear Veterans Vocational Rehabilitation Act.

1920 The Fess-Smith Civilian Vocational Rehabilitation Act, creating a vocational rehabilitation program for disabled civilians.

1920 24 states enact sterilization laws for people considered "mentally deffective."

1921 Department of Veteran Affairs established.

1922 The International Council for the Education of Exceptional Children is founded.

1924 Immigration Restriction Act limits immigration from Eastern and Southern Europe after testimony by Eugenicist Harry Laughlin who falsely determines that people from these regions have lower IQs.

1927 The U.S. Supreme Court rules in Buck vs. Bell that the compulsory sterilization of mental defectives is constitutional.

1932 Three quarters of the school districts in the U.S. are using intelligence tests to place children in tracks. Franklin Roosevelt is elected President. He is in a wheelchair due to polio.

1932 Margaret Bourke White is hired to photograph Letchworth Village, an institution in New York.

1933 New Deal provides social and economic opportunities for working people.

1935 300 members of the League for the Physically Handicapped stage a nine day sit-in in New York City to protest their WPA employment applications being stamped with "PH" for physically handicapped.

1935 Social Security Act.

1936 Children's Benevolent League founded in Washington state.

1937 March of Dimes is founded.

1939 World War II begins. Hitler enacts the Aktion T4, a "euthanasia" program designed to eliminate the physically and mentally handicapped or "life unworthy of life."

1941 Rosemary Kennedy, President John F. Kennedy's sister, is permanently institutionalized in Washington after a lobotomy fails to cure her life-long mental disability and aggressive behavior.

1945 GI Bill of Rights provides unprecedented education opportunities for returning veterans.

1946 The United Cerebral Palsy Association is founded

1946 The National Mental Health Foundation is founded by conscientious objectors who served as attendants at state mental institutions during World War II. It works to expose the abusive conditions at these facilities and becomes an early impetus in the push for deinstitutionalization.

1946 The Hill Burton Act funds the building of hospitals and institutions.

1947 Paralyzed Veterans of America is founded.

1948 The United Nations General Assembly adopts the Universal Declaration of Human Rights.

1948 Irving Haberman's photographs exposing the wretched and overcrowded conditions in an institution are published.

1950 The National Association for Retarded Children is founded.

1950 Popular novelist Pearl S. Buck writes *The Child Who Never Grew*, a memoir about her mentally retarded daughter.

1950 NARC, an advocacy group for parents with mentally retarded children, is formed in Minneapolis. The organization will develop branches worldwide.

1951 Institute for Rehabilitation Medicine in New York.

1952 With royalties from her book *Angel Unaware*, a book by about her retarded child, actress Dale Evans funds a national public awareness campaign.

1954 Brown vs. the Board of Education rules that "separate but equal" violates the 14th Amendment.

1954 The second week in November becomes National Retarded Children's Week.

1955 The Mental Health Study Act.

1960 Social Security Disability program is amended to allow people under 50 to qualify for benefits.

1961 John F. Kennedy appoints a presidential panel on mental retardation.

1961 Freedom Rides begin—campaign to end bus segregation.

1962 Findings of the Panel on Mental Retardation are published.

1962 Eunice Kennedy Shriver writes an article for the *Saturday Evening Post* about her sister Rosemary Kennedy who is mentally retarded.

1962 Jerome Lejuene discovers the chromosomal abnormality that causes Down Syndrome.

1962 Ed Roberts sues to gain admission to the University of California.

1962 James Meredith sues to gain admission to the University of Mississippi.

1963 Lyndon Johnson assumes Presidency after the assassination of John F. Kennedy.

1963 250,000 persons of all races demonstrate in Washington, D.C., in support of Civil Rights.

1963 Legislation providing basic research and training dollars for mental retardation is enacted and administered by the National Institutes of Health.

1964 The Civil Rights Act prohibits discrimination on the basis of race, religion, or national origin

1965 Bloody Sunday—Black Americans demonstrate for voting rights. Police use violence to stop them.

1965 Voting Rights Act.

1965 *Christmas in Purgatory*; Burton Blatt and Fred Kaplan publish a Photographic Essay on Mental Retardation, revealing inhumane conditions in state institutions.

1965 The Social Security Act is amended, establishing Medicare and Medicaid.

1968 Eunice Kennedy Shriver founds the Special Olympics.

1968 Architectural Barriers Act signed.

1971 Ed Roberts and his associates found The Center for Independent Living in Berkeley, California.

1971 Education for All (House Bill 90)—passed in Washington State.

1971 Parc v. Pennsylvania—this case strikes a state law prohibiting handicapped children from attending public schools.

1972 Geraldo Rivera's documentary "The Last Disgrace" about conditions in Letchworth Village airs on television.

1973 Section 504 of the Rehabilitation Act is enacted, prohibiting discrimination toward otherwise qualified people with disabilities by recipients of federal financial assistance.

1973 Urban Mass Transit Act.

1974 People First—First convention held in Oregon, largest organization of people with developmental disabilities. Founds first organization of and by people with disabilities.

1974 American Association for the Education of the Severely/Profoundly Handicapped is formed. Later this organization would change its name to TASH.

1975 Public Law 92-142, The Education for All Handicapped Children Act, is passed and becomes a federal law.

1975 American Coalition of Persons with Disabilities founded.

1977 Disability activists take over the HEW offices in San Francisco until regulations for Section 504 are signed by Secretary Joseph Califano. The action lasts for one month.

1984 The National Council for the Handicapped becomes a Federal Agency.

1986 The Air Carriers Act is passed.

1988 "Deaf President Now" protest at Gallaudet University—the first deaf president Dr. I. King Jordan.

1988 Fair Housing Act is amended to include people with disabilities.

1989 The first version of the American Disabilities Act is introduced in Congress.

1989 The Berlin Wall comes down, the 200th anniversary of the French Revolution, students defy soldiers in Tienamen Square.

1990 The Americans with Disabilities Act is passed in both houses of Congress.

1990 IDEA 94-142—Name change to Individuals with Disabilities Education Act

1998 The Fair Housing Act is amended to include two new classes of people, families with children and people with disabilities.

1998 Persion Gulf War Veterans Act

1999 U.S. Supreme Court upholds the Olmstead Act rejecting the State of Georgia's appeal to enforce the institutionalization of individuals with disabilities.

1999 The Work Incentives Improvement Act passed; enables people to work and still receive healthcare benefits.

2003 S.1394, the Money Follows the Person Act, is introduced in Congress allowing for funding to follow individuals out of institutions.

a t i o n

in Italy - Fr...
childrer polici...
wor - 40 mo...
growth
health su...

U.S. labor movement

1930 ARC (Seattle) *movemental prents that made reforms in institutions*

Eugenics / Sterilization / Fear of *in America + Europe*

SSI

KOREAN WAR

WORLD WAR I

Anti-V...

Special education →

100,000 Disabled people killed...

U.S. DEPRESSION

HOLOCAUST

m

SOVIET REVOLUTION

WORLD WAR II

League women...

sufferage movement

Women

1935 Soc. Cr. Act.

CANADA - Also initiated prog.ams

1915 Dr. Harry J. Haiselden begins a crusade opposing surgery for babies born defective and is brought to court in Chicago when he allows a baby to starve to death because it is born deformed due to its mother contracting typhoid fever during pregnancy.

1916 Eugenics Record Office produces intelligence tests for men inducted in the military and encourages sterilization for the "unfit." Eugenics campaigns against people of color and immigrants lead to passage of "Jim Crow" laws in the South and legislation restricting immigration by Southern and Eastern Europeans, Asians, Africans, and Jews.

1917 Smith-Hughs Veteran Vocational Education Act.

1918 The Smith-Sear Veterans Rehabilitation Act.

1920 The Fess-Smith Civilian Vocational Rehabilitation Act, creating a vocational rehabilitation program for disabled civilians.

1920 24 states enact sterilization laws for people considered "mentally deffective."

1921 Department of Veteran Affairs established.

1922 The International Council for the Education of Exceptional Children is founded.

1924 Immigration Restriction Act limits immigration from Eastern and Southern Europe after testimony by Eugenicist Harry Laughlin who falsely determines that people from these regions have lower IQs.

1927 The U.S. Supreme Court rules in Buck vs. Bell that the compulsory sterilization of mental defectives is constitutional.

1932 Three quarters of the school districts in the U.S. are using intelligence tests to place children in tracks. Franklin Roosevelt is elected President. He is in a wheelchair due to polio.

1932 Margaret Bourke White is hired to photograph Letchworth Village, an institution in New York.

1933 New Deal provides social and economic opportunities for working people.

1935 300 members of the League for the Physically Handicapped stage a nine day sit-in in New York City to protest their WPA employment applications being stamped with "PH" for physically handicapped.

1935 Social Security Act.

1936 Children's Benevolent League founded in Washington state.

1937 March of Dimes is founded.

1939 World War II begins. Hitler enacts the Aktion T4, a "euthanasia" program designed to eliminate the physically and mentally handicapped or "life unworthy of life."

1941 Rosemary Kennedy, President John F. Kennedy's sister, is permanently institutionalized in Washington after a lobotomy fails to cure her lifelong mental disability and aggressive behavior.

1945 GI Bill of Rights provides unprecedented education opportunities for returning veterans.

1946 The United Cerebral Palsy Association is founded

1946 The National Mental Health Foundation is founded by conscientious objectors who served as attendants at state mental institutions during World War II. It works to expose the abusive conditions at these facilities and becomes an early impetus in the push for deinstitutionalization.

1946 The Hill Burton Act funds the building of hospitals and institutions.

1947 Paralyzed Veterans of America is founded.

1948 The United Nations General Assembly adopts the Universal Declaration of Human Rights.

1948 Irving Haberman's photographs exposing the wretched and overcrowded conditions in an institution are published.

1950 The National Association for Retarded Children is founded.

1950 Popular novelist Pearl S. Buck writes The Child Who Never Grew, a memoir about her mentally retarded daughter.

1950 NARC, an advocacy group for parents with mentally retarded children, is formed in Minneapolis. The organization will develop branches worldwide.

1951 Institute for Rehabilitation Medicine in New York.

1952 With royalties from her book Angel Unaware, a book by about her retarded child, actress Dale Evans runs a national public awareness campaign.